'There are many major problems facing the world today. As David Jones argues in Who Cares Wins, business has both a responsibility and an opportunity to be part of the solution and should be a major force for good in helping to solve some of the most pressing problems of our time.'
Archbishop Emeritus Desmond Tutu

'Sharp, smart – and right!'
Bob Geldof KBE, musician and activist

'Great businesses are not just a force for good in our economy – they are a force for good in our society too. They have the power, the creativity and the enterprise to help us tackle some of the most pressing social challenges we face. As David Jones explains in this important book, in the future the success stories will be those businesses who truly recognise their role in the Big Society – who acknowledge the social as well as the economic value they have the power to create, and who realise the difference we all can make by the decisions that we take.'
British Prime Minister, The Right Honourable David Cameron

'David Jones captures one of the most compelling and consequential trends of our time: companies realising that by doing good, they can end up boosting their bottom lines, as well. Who Cares Wins convincingly makes the case that corporate America's embrace of good causes is no mere feel-good marketing ploy – it's the way of the future.'
Arianna Huffington, President and Editor-in-Chief, The Huffington Post Media Group

'In Who Cares Wins, David Jones makes the case that the biggest winners in business will be those that operate transparently and authentically. In a world that is more closely connected through social technologies, openness and speed must become core business principles. Jones' work will motivate and inspire you to play an integral role in that change.'
Sheryl Sandberg, Chief Operating Officer, Facebook

'Rarely has a title so brilliantly encapsulated the essence of a book. What you would expect perhaps of a clever ad man. Yet in Who Cares Wins David Jones shows that he is so much more: a visionary business leader who has glimpsed the future – and it doesn't belong to those advocating the tired old ways of doing business.
    The forces of change are all around us: digitally empowered citizens and socially conscious consumers; a planet in distress and governments unable – or unwilling – to rise collectively to the challenge. Business can, indeed must, be part of the solution. But it's going to take bold strokes, not limp gestures. That's why Unilever has committed to double its size while halving its environmental footprint. As Jones argues, initiatives like this are not just the right thing to do, but the only way to build successful and competitive businesses for the long term.'
Paul Polman, CEO, Unilever PLC

'No business can remain competitive, without driving every level of its business towards the concept of social responsibility. David Jones' book Who Cares Wins reveals the forces at work to the business leaders -i.e, the core principles and visionary insight they need to identify to make their businesses successful, and how the result will be a better society. This book is a great guide to see how business can be a significant partner in the transition to a more sustainable world.'
Professor Muhammad Yunus

'David Jones taps into a powerful emerging force that is shaping the future of business: that the need to consider social impact – and to seize the opportunity arising from it – will help to determine the winners and losers in tomorrow's business world. Good governance, transparency and good corporate citizenship have always been a part of our business model at NYSE Euronext because they are part of who we are and what we do. In this book, David Jones shows that in today's business world, a company's societal impact must be a critical consideration in order to achieve sustainable success.'
Duncan Niederauer, CEO, NYSE, Euronext

'This book could not have come at a better time. The challenges that the world is facing can only be solved if the business community starts to integrate its economic agenda with its social and environmental responsibilities.This book should give business leaders the confidence and faith that integrating their economic, social and environmental agenda makes excellent business sense as consumers of the future will in their brand choices also integrate their consumer choices with their social and environmental responsibilities.'
Tex Gunning, CEO, AkzoNobel Decorative Painting

'With Who Cares Wins, David Jones issues a real challenge to business leaders: focus not just on performance but on the broader impact of your business on society and our planet. His message that in the future business will have to do good to do well, is both timely and true.'
Rakesh Kapoor, CEO, Reckitt Benckiser

'David Jones' book provides clear evidence that in the future only those companies will prosper which respond to the expectations of all stakeholders.'
Professor Klaus Schwab, Founder and Executive Chairman, World Economic Forum

'A clear message for business leaders that success comes through value creation for all rather than value capture for a few.'
Jean-François van Boxmeer, Chairman of the Executive Board and CEO, Heineken

'This is a fine book, well written and clear, and the message is deeply refreshing – that moral issues count as much if not more than merely financial ones. Thank God for David Jones!'
John Simpson, author, journalist and BBC World Affairs Editor

Who Cares Wins

PEARSON

At Pearson, we believe in learning – all kinds of learning for all kinds of people. Whether it's at home, in the classroom or in the workplace, learning is the key to improving our life chances.

That's why we're working with leading authors to bring you the latest thinking and the best practices, so you can get better at the things that are important to you. You can learn on the page or on the move, and with content that's always crafted to help you understand quickly and apply what you've learned.

If you want to upgrade your personal skills or accelerate your career, become a more effective leader or more powerful communicator, discover new opportunities or simply find more inspiration, we can help you make progress in your work and life.

Pearson is the world's leading learning company. Our portfolio includes the Financial Times, Penguin, Dorling Kindersley, and our educational business, Pearson International.

Every day our work helps learning flourish, and wherever learning flourishes, so do people.

To learn more please visit us at: **www.pearson.com/uk**

Who Cares Wins

Why good business
is better business

David Jones

PEARSON

Harlow, England • London • New York • Boston • San Francisco • Toronto • Sydney • Auckland • Singapore • Hong Kong
Tokyo • Seoul • Taipei • New Delhi • Cape Town • São Paulo • Mexico City • Madrid • Amsterdam • Munich • Paris • Milan

PEARSON EDUCATION LIMITED

Edinburgh Gate
Harlow CM20 2JE
Tel: +44 (0)1279 623623
Fax: +44 (0)1279 431059
Website: www.pearson.com/uk

First published in Great Britain in 2012

© Euro RSCG Worldwide, LLC

The right of David Jones to be identified as author of this work has been
asserted by him in accordance with the Copyright, Designs and Patents
Act 1988.

Pearson Education is not responsible for the content of third-party
internet sites.

ISBN: 978-0-273-76253-9

British Library Cataloguing-in-Publication Data
A catalogue record for this book is available from the British Library

Library of Congress Cataloging-in-Publication Data
A catalog record for this book is available from the Library of Congress

All rights reserved. No part of this publication may be reproduced,
stored in a retrieval system, or transmitted in any form or by any
means, electronic, mechanical, photocopying, recording or otherwise,
without either the prior written permission of the publisher or a licence
permitting restricted copying in the United Kingdom issued by the
Copyright Licensing Agency Ltd, Saffron House, 6–10 Kirby Street,
London EC1N 8TS. This book may not be lent, resold, hired out or
otherwise disposed of by way of trade in any form of binding or cover
other than that in which it is published, without the prior consent of the
publisher.

All trademarks used herein are the property of their respective owners.
The use of any trademark in this text does not vest in the author or
publisher any trademark ownership rights in such trademarks, nor does
the use of such trademarks imply any affiliation with or endorsement of
this book by such owners.

10 9 8 7 6 5 4 3 2 1
16 15 14 13 12 11

Typeset in Melior LT 9pt by 3
Printed and bound in Great Britain by Ashford Colour Press Ltd,
Gosport, Hampshire

Imagine a world where the people who did the most good made the most money...

To Mum and Dad, for being such wonderful parents and for encouraging us to live our lives to the full. And look, I've written a book, I told you that 'A' in my English 'O' level wasn't a fluke.

To Alphonse, Agathe, Auguste, and Apolline, so that hopefully you will understand one day why Daddy travelled so much. And when you are old enough to read this and all I'm doing is lazing around on a beach, surfing and drinking fine red wine, you'll know that there was once a time when I had a proper job.

To Karine for all of your support, encouragement, help, advice, fun and above all understanding on our journey from London to Sydney to Paris to New York and beyond.

Thanks too, to all of the people who worked so tirelessly to help me make this book a reality: the amazing Kate Robertson, Louise Jack, Annette Stover, Patrick Armitage, Alex Sehnaoui, Ann O'Reilly, Nancy Wynne, Michael Hayman and Mark Cowne. To everyone who took part in the crowd sourcing of the cover and to Will Payovich for his winning design. And finally to Liz Gooster and all the team from Pearson.

Contents

7 The future: making a decent profit / 157

Preface

Six years ago, I was asked to speak at Advertising Age Idea Conference about redefining creativity. The key point of my speech was that if we really wanted to redefine creativity, then we should show how it can be used to create positive change and create good things in the world.

I was trying to define a different perspective to creativity from the commercial side. In our industry we are brilliant at using creativity to change people's behaviour, to get them to buy product A instead of product B. But you can also use creativity to change people's behaviours in ways that make the world a better place. I believe this is not only an opportunity but also an obligation for those of us in the creative industry and that we can use our talents to address some of the bigger issues facing the world.

But clearly the opportunities and obligations go far beyond my own industry. Today, consumers, customers, employees and now shareholders expect business to be more socially responsible. They are frustrated with how things are. They want change. These key stakeholders now have unprecedented amounts of information about you and your actions and they have been digitally empowered to punish those businesses that don't live up to their standards.

Social media is creating what I believe will be a bigger transformation for business than the arrival of television. Today, doors that were previously closed are being forced open. This is potentially a cause for concern for certain individual businesses but it's a great thing for business and the world in general because it is the driving force of consumer sentiment on social media that will compel business to live up to a new standard.

Because, in my view, social media and social responsibility are not separate subjects – they are in fact totally interlinked. In the coming decade, businesses that are the most socially responsible will be the most successful and will reap huge benefits from the power of social media, as employees, shareholders and consumers become passionate advocates for their brands and businesses.

The danger of being one of the companies punished by empowered consumers for failing to do the right thing far outweighs the downsides of changing to be a better business. Already major and substantial progress is being made. You can seize the opportunity to out-behave your competition.

Yes, there are a number of questions business leaders have. Will behaving in a socially responsible way make my business more successful and more profitable? Will my customers and consumers really reward me for this? Will my board? Will my shareholders? I am convinced they will. Social media has dramatically empowered people. And I believe that people are fundamentally good and will use this power to make the world a better place.

When I was returning from Boston last year, I dropped my wallet in the main Boston station. In the two hours of panic that followed as I tried to find it – my green card was in the wallet, without which I couldn't travel overseas and which takes a year to get a replacement – I spoke to several people and explained what had happened. Half of them said: 'Forget it, you'll never see your wallet again, people are basically dishonest.' The other half said: 'Don't worry, you'll get your wallet back; people are on the whole good.'

I got my wallet back.

Maybe that only served to enhance my natural optimism. But I genuinely believe that business is already moving in the right direction. That many of the world's political leaders are starting to act. That there are even signs of hope from our friends in the banking and finance industry. That, regardless, I believe the social consumer and especially the brilliant younger generation that is the Millennials will drive us all to change, maybe even faster than some of us are comfortable with.

And what if I am wrong? What is the worst case scenario of us heading down this path to a new, more socially responsible world?

Well, imagine the consequences of going off and making business better and creating a better world for nothing.

Publisher's acknowledgements

We are grateful to the following for permission to reproduce copyright material:

Dilbert cartoon p. 3 courtesy of http://thedilbertstore.com; press release on p.8 courtesy of Leroy Stick (www.worldglobalpr.com); Gatorade photo on p. 50 by Steve Boyle, courtesy of Gatorade.

Colour plates
Plate 1 courtesy of Corbis; Plates 2 and 5 courtesy of www.agencerea.com; Plate 3 courtesy of Jérôme Sessini, photographer; Plate 4 courtesy of Daniel Sims, photographer; Plates 6 and 7 courtesy of Martyn Hicks Photography; Plate 8 courtesy of Anthony Dodge, videographer.

In some instances we have been unable to trace the owners of copyright material, and we would appreciate any information that would enable us to do so.

Out-behaving the competition: why business now needs to do good to do well

It takes 20 years to build a reputation and 5 minutes to ruin it. If you think about that you'll do things differently.

Warren Buffett

A change of direction

Before the financial meltdown, the fastest-growing trend in business was the move towards social responsibility, and the economic crisis has only served to accelerate this. The world saw all too clearly that the ruthless pursuit of profit at all costs almost led to the total collapse of the global financial and economic system. Today, many businesses that understand that the philosophy of 'profit for profit's sake' is no longer the key to sustainable success are actively seeking to change how they operate. Doing well and doing good are no longer seen to be mutually exclusive.

Overall, the crisis has magnified consumers' expectations that companies should give back as much as they take. Their voice is already highly influential and will only become more so. Social media has given people an amazing tool to keep business honest, to share information and above all to create movements to support or bring down those businesses, leaders or governments that they do or don't 'like'. And all at dramatic speed.

There is overwhelming evidence that the way in which companies go about their business is becoming more important than ever. A study carried out in 2010 found that 86% of consumers believe it's important that companies stand for something other than profitability.[1] As this book will show, it's time for business to really take note.

This change in direction will not only mean that business does less harm but ultimately will do much more good. As a variety of examples in this book demonstrate, it also makes sound long-term financial sense. Doing the right thing does not mean sacrificing profits and, in fact, will protect companies in future.

The three ages of socially responsible business

While business is starting to take seriously the need to behave according to a different standard, it wasn't always so. Previously, a company's image was often its key concern rather than its reality. Words spoke larger than actions. If we examine the path that led modern business to this new reality, it can be broken down into three ages, which fit broadly into three consecutive decades.

> a company's image was often its key concern rather than its reality

The Age of Image, 1990–2000

The first age – the Age of Image – lasted from around 1990 to 2000. Businesses used the growing interest in how companies went about their affairs and what they stood for, especially in an environmental context, to create new communications strategies.

These were, on the whole, designed to establish or alter the image of their businesses in the consumer's mind – rather than genuinely changing how things were done. As the Dilbert cartoon says: 'We didn't do it to help the planet; we did it to look like the sort of company that cares about that sort of thing.'

The terms 'greenwashing' and 'nicewashing' were coined to describe cynical attempts by companies to mislead the public about their environmental performance and ethical commitments.

In 1992, Greenpeace published a ferocious report entitled 'The Greenpeace Book of Greenwash', which eviscerated companies including DuPont, General Motors, Shell and Dow Chemical, among others, for co-opting environmental terms and using them for their own ends. Despite this, some companies continued to cosmetically enhance their images with claims and marketing campaigns that did not necessarily reflect reality.

The Age of Advantage, 2000–2010

As consumers grew more and more vocal, and more digitally empowered, some of the smarter and more progressive companies realised that there could be genuine competitive advantage to be gained from really delivering on the promises of the Age of Image. And hence we saw the arrival of the second age – the Age of Advantage (2000–2010).

Here we saw companies setting about to genuinely make their business more socially responsible, in order to gain an edge. Walmart transformed its business during this period, as we will examine in detail later. Others, such as Marks & Spencer and Toyota, leapt ahead of their competitors by genuinely tackling their impact on the world around them. New companies that placed better business as a central tenet, such as Whole Foods and Burt's Bees, began to make a significant impact, delivering on consumers' expectations.

In the Age of Advantage, many business leaders recognised and accepted the need for business to change. In fact, almost three-quarters of business leaders (73%) questioned in a global study in 2010 believed in the edge corporate social responsibility gave them and even more (79%) accepted it as a business cost.[2] These findings underline the sound instincts of the business leaders who have led the way during the Age of Advantage.

The Age of Damage, 2010 to the present

I believe we are now heading into the third age – the Age of Damage. If the first age was about creating an image but not delivering on it, and the second age was about the genuine delivery by the few, then the third age is poised to be an era during which businesses that are not socially responsible will suffer damage as a result of this failure. Consumers now know more about companies and expect more of them. Not only that, they will now act against those that do not come up to their standards.

Unilever CEO Paul Polman is well aware of this: 'Those companies that wait to be forced into action or who see it solely in terms of reputation management or CSR will do too little too late and may not even survive,' he warns.

Polman is committed to improving Unilever's sustainability performance, but not at the expense of growth, and intends to double the size of the business whilst halving its environmental impact.

Polman's goals are seen by many to be ambitious, but they are also the symbol of a new era in which companies focus on both their results and the impact of those results. Other companies that have occupied this space in the past decade have seen clear benefits. General Electric says it has spent $5 billion in the first five years of Ecomagination, its programme to develop clean technologies for the future, but adds that a staggering $70 billion has already been generated. General Electric CEO Jeffrey Immelt says: 'Ecomagination is not an advertising ploy or marketing gimmick. GE wants to do this because it is right, but also we plan to make money while we do so.'

Marks & Spencer launched Plan A in 2007, making 100 commitments to tackle climate change, waste, raw materials, fairness throughout its supply chain and health issues over five years to 2012. The retailer anticipated investing £200 million over the period to achieve these targets but, according to its 'How We Do Business' reports, the plan has already broken even; in 2010 it added £50 million in profit and in 2011 a net benefit of £70 million. This in addition to an energy efficiency improvement of 23%, 94% of all waste from stores, offices and warehouses recycled and major progress in terms of sustainable sourcing.

Many smaller, and often more niche, companies have been successfully delivering on the growing desire from consumers for products sold by businesses with a conscience. USA-based outdoor clothing company Patagonia has had a pioneering approach to sustainability, employee care and social responsibility and is considered a model of ethical business.

Patagonia has become a heavy-hitter in its sector but could easily aspire to grow faster. Its inspirational founder, Yvon

Chouinard, says: 'Everybody tells me it's an undervalued company, that we could grow this business like crazy and then go public. Make a killing. But that would be against everything I've wanted to do. It would destroy everything I believe in.'[3]

The attitudes of leaders like Chouinard strike a chord within consumers that echoes their own concerns. These companies prove that ethical manufacture is possible and the evidence strengthens consumer demands that other companies do likewise. Their growing scale places further responsibility on established companies to put their own houses in order, which they will have to do if they are to prosper in the Age of Damage.

Poster child for an era

The company that is probably the poster child for the negative side of the three ages is BP. Now, of course, the oil extraction business is not easy. If we had to live without oil tomorrow, the world would grind to a complete halt. It's a tough and complex business without an easy solution to reduce our dependency. And one that has been further complicated by the earthquake and tsunami in March 2011 in Japan. That said, if you know you are operating in this kind of business, my feeling is that you don't need to change your logo to a green flower and try to position yourself as one of the most eco-friendly businesses in the world. You don't need to change your strapline to Beyond Petroleum, when the most cursory examination reveals that you are not beyond it in any meaningful way.

For BP, during the catastrophic fall-out from the Deepwater Horizon oil spill in the Gulf of Mexico in 2010, the three ages came full circle. A company that pushed very hard to change its image rather than its reality, was on the receiving end of vociferous criticism on every level, especially in social media, BP was put under the microscope and found it could get away with nothing. Not only did we see that their reality was a long way from the crispy-clean image they had been presenting, but we also saw that they were woefully ill-equipped to operate in the new world of radical transparency.

At the height of the oil spill drama a satirical Twitter account posing as @BPGlobalPR began tweeting sardonic messages highlighting BP's ham-fisted approach to the crisis. Posts such as 'Safety is our primary concern. Well, profits, then safety. Oh, no – profits, image, then safety, but still, it's right up there'[4] began appearing and went global in mere seconds, making BP a laughing stock on top of everything else. People were far more interested in the spoof posts of @BPGlobalPR than BP's official Twitter posts – the former had 190,000 followers and the latter just 18,000. This meant that every time someone carried out an online search for BP, the first results they saw were damning condemnations of BP.

The author, who called himself Leroy Stick, issued a press release (see page 8), which beautifully illustrated why businesses need to tackle these issues as a matter of urgency. Twitter and other social media are a virtual stick that consumers can use to punish misbehaving companies. It was Leroy Stick's humiliating jokes that everyone shared, not BP's clumsy excuses. Stick was followed avidly and his posts retweeted endlessly, proving that, in the world of social media, an individual can take on a big company. BP shares lost over half their value in the weeks following the spill, going from over $60 a share to under $30 a share in two weeks.

Dearest Media

My name is Leroy Stick and I am the man behind @BPGlobalPR. First, let me begin by explaining my name. When I was growing up, there was a dog that lived on my block named Leroy. Leroy was a big dog with a disdain for leashes and a thirst for blood. He made a habit of running around our block attacking anything he saw, biting my dad and my dogs basically whenever he had the chance. He chased me a few times, but I always escaped because I was/am an amazing tree climber.

Anyhoos, after Leroy's second or third attack on my dogs, it became clear that the police and Leroy's owner weren't going to do anything to stop him, so my dad took matters into his own hands and came up with a brilliant invention: the Leroy stick.

The Leroy stick was, you guessed it, a stick. My dad carried an axe handle and I carried a plunger handle. My dad told me two things about carrying the Leroy stick. First, if Leroy came near me or the dogs, I should hit him. Second, if I hit Leroy with my stick, I would not get in trouble. Was it legal? Probably not. Was it right? It sure felt like it. We set the example and soon a lot of our neighbors started carrying Leroy sticks as well. Soon enough, Leroy and his owner saw everyone carrying sticks and Leroy didn't run free anymore.

If you think the point of this story is to beat dogs with sticks, then I'm guessing you probably still think I work for BP as well.

The point of this story is that if someone is terrorizing your neighborhood, sometimes it's alright to grab a stick and take a swing. Social media, and in this particular case Twitter, has given average people like me the ability to use and invent all sorts of brand new sticks.

I started @BPGlobalPR, because the oil spill had been going on for almost a month and all BP had to offer were bullshit PR statements. No solutions, no urgency, no sincerity, no nothing. That's why I decided to relate to the public for them. I started off just making jokes at their expense with a few friends, but now it has turned into something of a movement. As I write this, we have 100,000 followers and counting. People are sharing billboards, music, graphic art, videos and most importantly information.

Why has this caught on? I think it's because people can smell the bullshit and sometimes laughing at it feels better than getting angry or depressed over it. At the very least, it's a welcome break from that routine. The reason @BPGlobalPR continues to grow is because BP continues to spew their bullshit.

I've read a bunch of articles and blogs about this whole situation by publicists and marketing folk wondering what BP should do to save their brand from @BPGlobalPR. First of all, who cares? Second of all, what kind of business are you in? I'm trashing a company that is literally trashing the ocean, and these idiots are trying to figure out how to protect that company? One pickledick actually suggested that BP approach me and try to incorporate me into their actual PR outreach. That has got to be the dumbest, most head-up-the-ass solution anyone could possibly offer.

Do you want to know what BP should do about me? Do you want to know what their PR strategy should be? They should fire everyone in their joke of a PR department starting with all-star Anne Womack-Kolto and focus on actually fixing the problems at hand. Honestly, Cheney's publicist? That's too easy.

BP seems to only care about maintaining their image so they can keep making money, two things we have blatantly avoided. I don't have an image and I'm not making any money AT ALL for myself. Every penny we make from the t-shirts goes to the Gulf Restoration Network. Just a few hours ago, we made our first official $10,000 donation to healthygulf.org from the money we've made selling the "bp cares" t-shirts in one week.

So what is the point of all this? The point is, FORGET YOUR BRAND. You don't own it because it is literally nothing. You can spend all sorts of time and money trying to manufacture public opinion, but ultimately, that's up to the public, now isn't it?

You know the best way to get the public to respect your brand? Have a respectable brand. Offer a great, innovative product and make responsible, ethical business decisions. Lead the pack! Evolve! Don't send hundreds of temp workers to the gulf just to put on a show for the President. Hire those workers to actually work! Don't dump toxic dispersant into the ocean just so the surface looks better. Collect the oil and get it out of the water! Don't tell your employees that they can't wear respirators while they work because it makes for a bad picture. Take a picture of those employees working safely to fix the problem. Lastly, don't keep the press and the people trying to help you away from the disaster, open it up so people can see it and help fix it. This isn't just your disaster, this is a human tragedy. Allow us to mourn so that we can stop being angry.

In the meantime, if you are angry, speak up. Don't let people forget what has happened here. Don't let the prolonged nature of this tragedy numb you to its severity. Re-branding doesn't work if we don't let it, so let's hold BP's feet to the fire. Let's make them own up to and fix their mistakes NOW and most importantly, let's make sure we don't let them do this again.

Right now, PR is all about brand protection. All I'm suggesting is that we use that energy to work on human progression. Until then, I guess we've still got jokes.

Love,

Leroy Stick (aka a guy in his boxer shorts)

Influence epidemic

It is my firm belief that social media will be a potent
driver of social responsibility and positive social change in
years to come, influencing the behaviours of individuals,
corporations and governments.

In the old world, being an agent of change meant significant
effort, discomfort and even danger. At the very least, it
certainly necessitated leaving the house. Today you can take
part in a movement in the time it takes to become a fan, click
on 'like', upload a video or share a link. Cynics often dismiss
this as 'slacktivism' and claim that it is meaningless and,
of course, some of it is, but we have seen again and again
that the technology links activists with the rest of the world,
allows them to find supporters and amplifies their cause.

> those who dismiss social networks as
> platforms for inane chatter are really
> missing the significance of the changes
> taking place in the world today

In my view, those who dismiss social networks as platforms
for inane chatter are really missing the significance of the
changes taking place in the world today. In the aftermath of
the disastrous earthquake and tsunami in Japan, US specialists
went in to help with IT and technology issues. When internet
bandwidth was needed, a number of Japan's largest websites
were closed. Despite the bandwidth it was using, Facebook was
kept open because it was acting as an invaluable tool, helping
people make connections and find those who were missing.

There are countless instances where social media has served
a meaningful and even vital purpose. At Davos in 2011,
the now Minister of Infrastructure and Transport, Yassine

Brahim told the story of how during the Tunisian revolution people were using Facebook and Twitter to publish the locations of snipers in Tunis and other towns, both to keep other demonstrators out of the area and to pass on the word to the army who were trying to track down the snipers.

> there are countless instances where social media has served a meaningful and even vital purpose

Politicians and leaders of every kind are discovering social media is a great tool for connecting them to people, following the lead of President Obama, whose election campaign is probably the best example of a politician leveraging the power of social media.

Looking at the enormous shifts currently under way, I see two groups leading the charge: prosumers and the Millennial generation. The former are defined by attitudes and behaviours; the latter, by birth year – yet both are fuelling the rise in social activism that will define these times.

The Millennials form the most socially responsible generation that has ever existed. It is their voice that is the biggest accelerator of the global movement toward a more socially responsible future.

Today's young people are the ones who will have to live with the results of climate change. They are the ones who will be saddled with the debts incurred by previous generations. And they intend to do something about it, for they know with grim certainty that their elders have proved incapable.

In a global survey of Millennials, 84% agreed it is their generation's 'duty' to change the world, with a high of 90% agreement in China. Almost as many, 82%, believe their generation has the power to bring about positive global change.[5] And the source of that power is social media.

Another unique aspect of this generation is their view on privacy, as community manager for Crowd Media, James Bougourd explains below.

Privacy is Dead

Privacy is an odd concept to my generation. Ever since my teens every tiny detail about my life has been shared with the world. This might worry a concerned parent to death, but I didn't care then and I still don't now.

MySpace was the first social network to get me hooked. When I started it was a bit of a 'who has the most friends' contest. This meant that almost anyone could view everything I was putting online. When Facebook came along I was a lot savvier, I still didn't mind who was looking at my profile but I had a much more select group of friends.

Fast forward to today, and I'm sharing a lot more about myself than I was even when I was using MySpace. Using a mixture of Twitter, YouTube, Facebook and Foursquare, my friends can see what I'm doing at work, where I'm going for lunch, and what I'm thinking about all day. This is what I'm used to, I grew up with the foundations of this technology.

So why am I so relaxed about people seeing what I do online? Because I'm not an idiot.

Recently a woman was fired from her job for ranting about her boss on Facebook.

There have been countless stories about similar incidents and I have the same feelings about every one.

'Don't say anything online that you wouldn't want plastered on a billboard with your face on it.' (*Erin Bury, Sprouter Community Manager*)

This quote by Erin Bury says it all. If I don't want someone to know something about me, I don't put it online. As it happens I'm very much an open person and I don't have many secrets, but if I did, I wouldn't shout about them on the internet, just as I wouldn't shout about them in real life.

The second group of people driving change are prosumers. They are consumers who are more influential, more engaged, more knowledgeable and more cynical of marketing. I will talk more about them in Chapter 2.

But it isn't just Millenials and prosumers driving change. Technology has dramatically empowered everybody and given them the ability to act and influence others. And, ordinary people actually believe they have the power to effect positive change. Spurred by frustration and disillusionment, armed with more information than ever and empowered by their connections to one another, they are collectively insisting that the world become a better place.

What this means for businesses, in my view, is that the only profitable path to the future is one that is in a fairer and more sustainable direction.

Putting social responsibility at the core of business strategy

Genuinely making a business more socially responsible is hard work and affects every single aspect of a company, from how employees are treated, to action on local and global environments, to sharing and caring with local and global communities. It's not a case of simply giving generously or acting correctly in isolation; an entire business cannot simply be 'nicewashed'. Social responsibility must be at the core of business strategy.

Walmart has put itself through this process and is reaping the benefits. In the first half of the decade Walmart was losing as many as 8% of shoppers because of its poor reputation.[6] Expectations of business were rising and Walmart was failing to meet them.

In 2005, Walmart's then chief executive, Lee Scott, made a pivotal speech to the company's employees that set out numerous ambitious goals. These included increasing the efficiency of the vehicle fleet, one of the biggest in the USA, within three years and to double efficiency within 10 years; to eliminate 30% of the energy used in stores; to reduce solid waste by 25% within three years … the list goes on.

Big is good

The Baby Boomer generation was brought up to generally believe that big is bad, and this presents an exciting challenge: to prove that big companies can have a positive impact on society. I believe that we are entering an era in which some of the world's biggest companies will prove that big can be good. In fact, on many levels, the bigger you are, the more positive an impact you can have – as One Young World Counsellor, Doug Richard says, 'You can't share a loss', so the more successful you are, the more of an impact you can have. The reason that Bill Gates and Warren Buffett have been able to have a genuine impact with their philanthropy is that they had $40 billion to give away in the first place. I think it will also be an era in which 'big is good' will be applied not only to those major global companies who are doing the right thing, but also to the mass movements of people driving them down this path – the 'big' groups of people, making 'big' business 'good'.

There are many smaller companies that have also placed environmental friendliness and social responsibility at the core of business strategy and, in some cases, as their raison d'être. While their philosophical impact is influential, their physical impact is comparatively small.

Naturally, it is a lot simpler to start a company from scratch than to adapt and modernise a major global business that may be entrenched in supply chain relationships and committed to technologies that need updating. But it is only when the major global corporations of the world act and change that we will see a real impact.

Put another way, not that many people care what Luxembourg is doing to address the issue of global climate change, but everyone wants to know what steps China and the USA are taking.

Walmart's actions matter – Scott knew that if Walmart could influence just a fraction of its 1.8 million employees or 176 million weekly customers, the impact would be huge. Furthermore, the clout the company wields with its suppliers would mean that business practices throughout the USA would have to change. Scott admits the campaign started out as a defensive strategy, but it has turned out to be precisely the opposite. During his 2005 speech, Scott said: 'We will not be measured by our aspirations. We will be measured by our actions.' What can also be measured are the tangible benefits.

When you are the world's largest company you are going to have enemies, and Walmart continues to be criticised on a number of levels, notably because of several legacy employee class actions. Yet there are few companies that have taken such major steps towards becoming a more socially responsible business, and Walmart's actions have had a greater impact on making the USA's and the world's supply chain more sustainable than any other company's.

Transforming a business from its core is an admittedly complex and demanding path to walk. But not only is it the right thing to do; the business case for it is also becoming as apparent as the dangers of ignoring it. The critical factor in these transformations is leadership, which we explore in Chapter 3. It isn't easy, but the rewards are worth it.

Radical transparency

If I had to pick one word to use as the guideline for running a business in this new era, it would be 'transparency'. And the research among business leaders, where 67% believe that business success is based in corporate transparency, supports this. Businesses that are transparent, authentic and fast will be better on every level and in a stronger position to face the Third Age.

In the old world, the people who had the most power were those who had the most information. They kept this information to themselves, except when it served their purposes to do otherwise. Large institutions could tell different people different things; investors, employees and consumers were given different messages that could be kept distinct from each other. This is no longer possible because now everyone can see everything.

And, as we enter a new decade, the tables have turned: now the people who have the most power are those who share the most. Information is everywhere and can be accessed by virtually anyone. Hypocrisy and inconsistency are sure to be found out. Anonymity is not an option.

In an illustration of the importance of transparency, Walmart publishes not only those targets it reaches but also those it misses.[7] The result is that its efforts come across as honest and authentic.

Transparency is a relatively new concept for business, but it has become hugely important in recent years – and the pressures behind it are definitely not going away. Among prosumer, or, influential consumer, respondents to a survey,[8] 82% say they know more these days about the companies that make the products and services they use.

In part, that is because they are going out and seeking this information: in the few months before the survey, 62% of prosumers and 41% of mainstream consumers had actively looked for information on the reputation or ethics of a company. Seven in ten prosumers surveyed say that by making everything more open and transparent, social media is making the world a better place.

Act before somebody acts on your behalf

In the new era of transparency and consumer empowerment, it is far better for brands to initiate the conversation than to pick up on it halfway through, to take the lead rather than be led, to contribute voluntarily rather than be pulled into a futile attempt at defence. And authenticity trumps image every time.

> it is far better for brands to initiate the conversation than to pick up on it halfway through

Nike was one of the first companies to learn that today if a company does not act on its own behalf to be operationally transparent, it may find that someone else will act for it.

In 2005 Nike made an early move towards openness after being heavily criticised for years for not doing enough to tackle poor working conditions along its supply chain.

Nike founder Phil Knight admitted the company had been slow to react to evidence of bad practice and responded by publishing the addresses of all its contracted factories. The aim was to provide a complete picture and, at the time, Nike said its goal was to be as accurate, complete and honest as it could be about how it operates.

Nestlé learned a hard lesson when it was attacked for its part in the deforestation of Indonesian rainforests, threatening animals with extinction in order to make way for palm oil plantations.

The power of social media proved apparent as support grew behind campaigns demanding Nestlé change its ways. For example, a YouTube video by Greenpeace called 'Have a Break?' – parodying ads for Nestlé product Kit Kat – spread rapidly around the world.

Nestlé compounded its misery by badly mishandling comments on its own Facebook page; the company was pursued by the online community and the story blew up into a barrage of global criticism, on- and offline. As a result (and one that was a notable victory for social media), at the time of writing Nestlé had cancelled a contract with a palm oil supplier as part of its response.

Social media has also changed the role of activists and non-governmental organisations (NGOs) such as Greenpeace. Historically, when business or governments acted poorly, it was these groups that confronted them. The Kit Kat video shows that when NGOs create content that people want to share, a message can gain the kind of momentum needed to really make a difference.

In recent years there has been a trend towards collaborative relationships between NGOs and corporations, like that of Greenpeace and Unilever who after a long battle over deforestation as a result of palm oil production have latterly been working in partnership. This may be indicative of the new era of collaboration and cooperation, that is permeating society on so many levels.

I do hope so. One of my personal concerns is that as business moves to be more socially responsible, rather than embracing this movement the NGOs step away from business, believing their role is to be the moral compass for business rather than to effect positive change in the world. This would be a shame as I think that both can learn a lot from each other. Historically, the NGOs had great intentions but often not great execution. The world of business had great execution but often not great intentions. In the twenty-first century the key to success is to deliver on both.

Caveat: the customer isn't always right

What happens on social networks matters, and it is only going to become more significant. But this does not mean that tweeters and bloggers are always right. Often discussions online are unfair and misleading – intentionally or otherwise.

As a parent of four children under the age of eight, I am no stranger to nappies, or diapers as I now have learnt to call them. So I took an interest when a group of mums started a Facebook page to bring back Pampers Cruisers, which had been replaced by Pampers Dry Max.

What caught my interest were the claims on the page that the new nappies were causing chemical burns on infants' skin – not what a parent wants to hear about a trusted brand. What is interesting about this case is that what started out as a bunch of people annoyed that Procter &

Gamble had switched products without notice morphed into a group of very angry parents laying all sorts of accusations against the P&G nappies without backup from the medical community.

Indeed, once lawsuits were filed and the US Consumer Product Safety Commission decided to investigate, the commission ended up exonerating Dry Max, saying there was no evidence of chemical burns and that the product wasn't any more prone to cause rashes than any other nappy brand. But by that time the Pampers Bring Back the Old Cruisers Facebook page had attracted more than 11,000 fans and spread the 'news' around the world that the new product posed a serious health threat to babies. The debate continued online and, I presume, offline in homes and playgrounds.

Even when a brand is not engaged in any wrongdoing, which would seem to be the case with P&G and Pampers Dry Max, it can be incredibly difficult to defend oneself against impassioned detractors in the social media space. There will always be instances of false accusations, biased reviews and undisclosed conflicts of interest. Also, people will allow inconsistencies in themselves and their peers that they will not tolerate in businesses.

The best thing to do is to remain open and honest, and to communicate in good faith with all those who have an issue with your brand. You won't win over every detractor, but at least you won't be creating new ones by the way you are responding to consumer-critics.

Out-behaving the competition

So what of those people who say that socially responsible business is just a short-term, recession-driven fad? Or that no one has succeeded in both being good and making money?

There is a growing body of evidence that demonstrates that it is a path that many stakeholders want business to go down. Consumers understand they can control companies through their purchasing behaviour. They also realise that, in many respects, they have more power and control of companies than they do over governments.

A major global study found that three-quarters (74%) of consumers think that business bears as much responsibility for driving positive social change as governments.[9] This supports my view that Milton Friedman's assertion in the 1970s that business's only responsibility is to maximise profits for shareholders, and therefore social responsibility is anti-business, is now obsolete.

For an increasing number of business leaders today, earlier conflicts between doing the right thing and making a profit no longer exist. The erosion of the Friedman argument has come about as a natural evolution, enabled by our growing interconnection, spurred by the economic meltdown, as well as a widening acknowledgement of the plight of our planet and its inhabitants.

The endorsement of business's wider moral responsibility is reflected in the Giving Pledge, a promise made by 40 billionaires, led by Bill Gates and Warren Buffet, to give at least half of their fortunes to charity. Buffet and Gates are targeting a further 360 billionaires. If they secure pledges from the 400 richest people in the USA, the total pledged would amount to $600 billion.

This is straightforward philanthropy, of course, and arguably provoked by guilt, but it sets a tone for business and business leaders as to how they are supposed to behave.

The Millennial generation in particular cares strongly about behaviour and also the motivations behind it. They will not be satisfied with charitable donations made in the twilight of stellar careers – they want business to behave better right now. They are not opposed to business making money; they just demand that it is done in the right way. And in fact, in my view, it will become very difficult for a business to succeed and become big if it doesn't behave the right way from day one.

Millennials believe strongly that we are all in this together and this moral interdependence is one of the keys to competitive advantage in the Age of Damage. As the BP drama unfolded, it was clear who was to blame and how they reacted and handled the crisis became almost as important as what had actually happened.

This aspect will become increasingly significant – more and more, business and its leaders will be judged on their very intentions and how they react to the issues that confront them. For those that get it wrong, social media will prove a very public and powerful people's court. If this generation of young people can topple previously immovable dictatorships, as we have seen across the Arab world, then imagine what they can do to your brand.

With more than three-quarters (80%) of consumers believing that they have the responsibility to censure unethical companies by avoiding their products,[10] the punishment for those falling short will be harsh.

Democratised information has led to democratised power, and a new balance is at work. But this does not spell the end of successful profitable businesses or indeed the death of capitalism but instead the birth of a new green-blooded capitalism.

Summary: being the company you want to keep

▌ The true cost of the pursuit of profit for profit's sake is too high.

▌ In the world of radical transparency, reality is more important than image.

▌ Today, the people who have the most power are those who share the most.

▌ Millennials and prosumers will not only change the world; they will change the way in which the world changes.

▌ Transparency, authenticity and speed are the rules of modern business.

▌ Social responsibility needs to be at the core of business strategy, not in a silo.

▌ Smart companies will out-behave their competitors – and act before someone acts on their behalf.

▌ Social responsibility and social media are intrinsically linked – in fact, social responsibility drives social media.

▌ 'Big is good' will be the mantra for the successful corporation in the twenty-first century.

▌ The most successful businesses in the future will be those that are the most socially responsible.

References

1   Havas, *Social Business Study* (2010), New York, Market Probe International.

2   Havas, *Socially Responsible Business Study* (2010), London, YouGovStone.

3   Susan Casey, 'Patagonia: blueprint for green business', *Fortune* (2007), http://money.cnn.com/magazines/fortune/fortune_archive/2007/04/02/8403423/index.htm.

4   http://thetweetwatch.com/Detail/Status/15504031663

5   Euro RSCG Worldwide, *Millenials Study* (2010), New York, Market Probe International.

6   Michael Barbaro, 'A new weapon for Wal-Mart: a war room', *New York Times* (2005), www.nytimes.com/2005/11/01walmart.ready.html?emc=eta1.

7   'Sustainability Commitments, Goal 2: Create Zero Waste' in Walmart 2010 Sustainability Progress Report, p. 35.

8   Havas, *Social Business Study* (2010), New York, Market Probe International.

9   Ibid.

10 Ibid.

The new world of marketing: creating a successful brand in a dramatically changing world

You know the best way to get the public to respect your brand? Have a respectable brand.

Leroy Stick aka @BPGlobalPR

Someone changed the questions

If the world of business has entered a new and dramatically changed environment, then the changes and challenges confronting the marketing world have been even more dramatic. The 'social' consumer is driving business to be more socially responsible.

An industry that has spent decades perfecting the answers to the key marketing questions is waking up to the fact that those questions have suddenly changed.

As Chapter 1 explained, we are living in an open world where transparency and authenticity are the most important values; where people can and will find out everything about your brand and share it with each other; where consumers

> we are living in an open world where transparency and authenticity are the most important values

want to know what a company or brand stands for; and where brands are defined by what consumers say to each other about them, not what the brand says to consumers.

This is the new playground for the Social Brand. It's changing the rules of the marketing world. It offers enormous opportunity for those who get it right, and a very fast and public humiliation for those who don't.

So how should marketers react in this new world to create successful and trusted brands?

Leroy Stick aka @BPGlobalPR provides a very succinct answer – 'You know the best way to get the public to respect your brand? Have a respectable brand.' This should be the mantra for every marketer in the coming decade. For today's consumers, actions really do speak louder than words. And I would argue that if in the past century we built brands through marketing, then in this one we will build them through behaviour.

For those looking for a slightly more in-depth answer than Mr Stick's, the following ten points represent my views on the key changes taking place and guidelines for creating successful brands in the social age.

1 From image is everything to reality is everything

One of the biggest global TV hits of the past few years has been *Mad Men* – a programme about the birth of consumerism in the traditional advertising world, which aired primarily on 'traditional' media. Not only does the success of this show help to make the point that so-called traditional media is not yet dead, but it is also a great demonstration of a major change I want to cover, which is the shift from a world of image to a world of reality.

The marketer's job used to be about creating the best possible image for any product. No matter how divorced from the truth that image might have been.

Consider the signature 'It's toasted'. It sounds like the slogan for a delicious and nutritious food product. But the following exchange from the above-mentioned TV show reveals it is anything but:

Don Draper: *This is the greatest advertising opportunity since the invention of cereal. We have six identical companies making six identical products. We can say anything we want. How do you make your cigarettes?*

Lee Garner, Jr.: *I don't know.*

Lee Garner, Sr.: *Shame on you. We breed insect-repellent tobacco seeds, plant them in the North Carolina sunshine, grow it, cut it, cure it, toast it.*

Don Draper: *There you go. There you go.*

[Writes on chalkboard and underlines: 'IT'S TOASTED.']

Lee Garner, Jr.: *But everybody else's tobacco is toasted.*

Don Draper: *No. Everybody else's tobacco is **poisonous**. Lucky Strike's ... is **toasted**.*

Don Draper's line, 'We can say anything we want', may have been a mantra for marketers and advertisers in the past century, but we now live in a world where reality, not image, is everything.

Naomi Klein's best-selling book *No Logo* purported that people would no longer be interested in brands. Whether you buy into that theory or not – and I personally don't, as I think in a world of more and more messages, shorter and shorter attention spans and smaller and smaller screens, brands will become more not less important to navigate the clutter – the one thing that is certain today is that consumers are increasingly interested in the company behind the brand and what that company believes in and stands for.

In today's open world, it's incredibly difficult for a company to pretend it is something it is not. Someone, somewhere, will find out and share that with the world. They are now interested in who makes the products they buy.

So far from 'saying anything' and creating a great image for your product or company, the key to today's successful social brand is to create or identify the best possible reality and share that with as many people as possible and to actually make that reality better in the first place.

Perhaps the best recent example of reality in marketing is the Domino's Pizza campaign in North America. We will cover that in more depth in the next chapter on leadership, but what Domino's did went against every previous marketing convention. Rather than hide the research that said that people thought their products tasted really bad – with consumer comments ranging from 'like cardboard' to 'not much love in that' – they shared them with the entire world in their television advertising and used them as the platform for a very successful turnaround. And in the next development of their campaign, they actually started showing the food in their advertising the way it really looks, rather than spending hours prepping and heavily retouching it to look amazing. The approach seems to be working. At the time of writing, same-store sales have grown 14% year on year. Proof that honesty really is the best policy.

Another great example is the Dulux Let's Colour campaign. Let's Colour is the platform for Dulux's bigger-picture mission to bring colour to brighten up grey spaces around the world – the creative execution of it was to actually engage the local communities in poor areas of Rio in Brazil, Jodhpur in India, and London and Paris and to film them painting depressing and dreary places with bright vibrant colour. This real footage, of real people, painting real places was then shared with the world.

Reality doesn't just extend to marketing communications, however. It extends to every area of the mix. For those people worried that their reality isn't quite as good as they would like, they needn't be. Today's social consumer is more interested in honesty than perfection. Walmart and Marks & Spencer, as we saw in Chapter 1, are completely transparent in reporting how they are performing against numerous ethical targets they have set themselves. When they fail, they say by how much and what they are going to do about it. This gives much greater credibility to the things that they say they have accomplished.

Other companies, such as Starbucks, are now following this template of honesty in their reporting around social responsibility. Businesses that seek to gloss over or omit where they have fallen short will be regarded as dishonest. The digitally empowered prosumer who decides he or she doesn't like what a business is doing is to be feared – and actually, I would argue, much more so than regulatory bodies. Advertising and communications campaigns can be hijacked in a single click and turned into a liability rather than an asset, as the Chevron case study on p. 30 demonstrates.

It's not just oil companies such as Chevron and BP that are likely to fall foul of this kind of action. Any campaign that is out of step with reality provides ample opportunity for consumer criticism and even for spoofs to emerge and be spread though social media.

CASE STUDY

When image does not = reality

In October 2010 oil company Chevron, owner of Texaco, hoped to convince the public it was on side with everything ordinary people believe. 'We agree' press ads declared in response to statements such as 'Oil companies should put their profits to good use' and 'Oil companies should support the communities they are part of' and, ironically, 'Oil companies should get real'.

Even in the unlikely event that the populace would be captivated by such a campaign, it was for nothing as it was elaborately subverted by the Yes Men, a pair of activists whose darkly comic high-jinks with a serious point have been directed at the likes of Dow Chemical and the World Trade Organization in the past. These two social activists have a thorough understanding of social media and create and maintain convincing fake websites as part of their activities.

A Chevron website was faked at www.chevron-weagree.com, with fake ads such as 'Oil companies should clean up their messes ... We agree' displayed as if they were the real thing.

The serious point behind the satire was that Chevron was fighting a legal case in Ecuador, where it was accused of failing to repair damage caused by its oil fields there.

Convincing press releases and the spoof versions of the campaign were sent out to credulous journalists just before the Chevron campaign launched. Fake stories using copies of publications' mastheads were also produced.

Overall the campaign backfired on Chevron. It was another example of the need to avoid nicewashing, to be genuine, and, above all, to underpromise and to overdeliver.

2 From consumers to prosumers

The key driver in this change from image to reality is the changing consumer. We're increasingly moving into a world where prosumers, or influential, proactive, marketing savvy, engaged consumers, are much more important.

On a simplistic level, the old world of marketing was somewhat linear. It was a straight-line relationship between brand and consumer and a simple matter of a brand pushing an ad at a fairly captive audience sitting immobile in front of their televisions. But if the old world of marketing was linear, the new world of marketing is square.

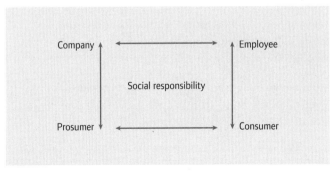

FIGURE 2.1

As you can see in Figure 2.1, in the top-left corner of
the square sits the company, in the bottom-left corner
the prosumer, in a third corner the consumer and in the
final corner the employee. The basic principle of Square
Marketing™ is as follows: if a brand or business is sufficiently
compelling, engaging and motivating to consumers, those
consumers will become proactive consumers, or prosumers,
and act as influential advocates for that brand. Conversely, if
they disagree with what the brand or business does or stands
for, they will have a similarly influential but negative impact.

The same applies for employees. They now have an ability
to be a truly powerful force for a company – or not. As I
cover later, they also can accidentally be a negative force
working against the company.

Now, none of this is actually new. Consumers could always
say things to other consumers, and employees could always
be positive or negative about the companies they worked for.
What is new is that social media has dramatically changed the
scale, velocity and impact of these conversations. In the old
marketing world, prosumers could influence a few people. In
the new world, depending upon their level of influence, they
can influence hundreds, thousands or even millions of people.

A global study from 2008 showed that 20% of people had
changed their minds about a product or service because
of a non-branded blog or forum.[1] Asked the same question
in 2010, the percentage in agreement had shot up to 41,
including 65% of prosumers.[2]

Lots of marketers now understand this and they and
their agencies set out to achieve a viral success, using the
potential power of digital movement.

Around the world clients are briefing their agencies, saying:
'I'd really like one of those viral ads that becomes a massive

global hit please.' The harsh reality is that the majority of 'viral' videos don't go viral. Too often companies put their latest TV ad on YouTube and wait for something to happen. It almost certainly won't. The fact that 90% of branded virals fail to generate any buzz whatsoever according to the World Advertising Research Centre (Warc) is a sobering one.

The reason for this is that the process of creating content that people want to share is part art, part science. And the process of seeding it is exactly the same. The key is to create content that is compelling. An idea that is social. A creative process that is social. And a brilliantly innovative media strategy to ensure the idea becomes contagious. We call this Social Creativity™.

Evian Roller Babies is currently in the Guinness Book of Records as the most downloaded piece of commercial content in history. It has now surpassed 180 million downloads and won the 2010 Grand Effie, an award judged solely on sales effectiveness. The process of creating this viral hit involved a very deliberate and calculated social media strategy. It was much more than just posting a film on to the internet and hoping the rest would take care of itself.

If Evian is an example of the positive impact of millions of prosumers, then BP is an example of the power and disruption of a single prosumer. Influential consumers don't always act as a supporter of a company – sometimes they will act against it. As we saw in Chapter 1, the individual using the alias Leroy Stick garnered 190,000 followers on his spoof Twitter feed, @BPGlobalPR. This dwarfed the 18,000 or so followers the global might of BP could muster. Stick not only lit up the Twittersphere; the story was widely covered in other media channels, proving the important and influential role of Twitter.

If the rules for the past century were about giving advice to the all-powerful brand on how to better interact with people, so the rules for this century are about how a brand needs to behave to ensure it doesn't attract the wrath of the all-powerful consumer. David Ogilvy in his 1963 book *Confessions of an Advertising Man* famously said, 'The consumer isn't a moron, she's your wife.' We need to update that saying for today to be 'The consumer isn't a moron. She's digitally empowered, marketing-savvy and highly influential and can bring down your brand in a matter of minutes.'

Seller beware!

While many of us would wholeheartedly support and endorse what Leroy Stick did, it's not always the case that prosumers criticise companies based on legitimate grounds. In the open world, controlling what people say is not possible; and there are no guarantees that they will say something good or something that reflects well on a brand.

As we saw in the Pampers example in Chapter 1, sometimes consumer criticism is unfair. It is never going to be easy to deal with unfair comments, but the key is to be honest, to provide as much information as you can and move very, very fast.

Similarly, while you may like a new product idea or logo design, people may not. On 6 October 2010, Gap launched a new logo in an attempt to create a more modern look for the brand. There was a huge backlash against the new logo in social media, with negative campaigns on Facebook and across Twitter, and even a www.craplogo.me website that asked 'Why hire an expensive firm when you can create a crap logo instantly using this site?' In a major U-turn, Gap returned to its previous logo only one week after the new logo's debut, and Marka Hansen, the person who had overseen the logo change, resigned soon after.

3 From employees to advocates

In the world of Square Marketing it isn't only prosumers who have an incredibly enhanced ability to influence. Employees, who sit at the top right-hand side of the square, can be a highly positive or negative force for a brand too.

If they believe passionately in a business and brand, they will become powerful advocates. This is particularly relevant given the fact that many people entering the workforce today would actually work at a company whose values they believed in for a lower salary than at a higher-paying competing firm they viewed to be less socially responsible.

Best Buy's Twelpforce and online retailer Zappos are often held up as top examples of employee engagement – both companies put in place systems that allow their employees to use Twitter to respond to customer service questions, creating a win-win: happier customers, and more involved and engaged employees. There are an ever-growing number of examples of companies following suit and empowering their employees using social media.

Not only can employees have an amazingly positive influence, but also social media in general, and Twitter specifically, can be used to dramatically improve customer service and interactions. Kodak, using a prescient name for its range of digital cameras, EasyShare, embraced social media, building a real-time relationship with consumers and product users. Its then chief marketing officer Jeffrey Hayzlett stated that the main aim initially was to enable customers to reach the company with complaints, but it has developed into much more than that. Now users share ideas, tips and suggestions and Kodak gets far more of these than it does complaints.

Social media is not only a space where employees can both talk and listen; employees can also sell. Dell is one of several companies making money out of Twitter and is attributing a rising number of sales to it.

Dell's experience in social media has been hard won, finding itself on the end of heavy criticism in 2005 from bloggers and prosumers for dreadful service. A well-known blogger, Jeff Jarvis, in an open letter to CEO Michael Dell, invited him to join the conversation that was taking place without him. He did, famously admitting, 'We screwed up, right?'

Interestingly, as Dell's followers on Twitter have grown, its sales have not grown in the same proportion. This suggests that from a purely sales perspective it may be better to have a smaller audience of people genuinely interested in buying a product, than a larger audience of less commercially engaged people. That said, there are obvious benefits from having a greater absolute number of followers, beyond sales alone.

In order to really leverage employee efforts, it is important to genuinely embrace social media rather than keep it in a remote silo where a lone brave employee dips his or her toe into the water of the social world like an intrepid explorer. Or where a PR specialist is engaged to try out social media on behalf of a company, at arm's length. It really can't be done in isolation – as we see in the Eurostar example below.

CASE STUDY

It can't be done in isolation

If Channel Tunnel train service Eurostar had thought to integrate its social media activity, it would have had the ability to deal with the weather-driven crisis in services in December 2009 in real time directly with its passengers, and it could have saved itself and its customers a whole lot of heartache. When five trains broke down in the freezing conditions, 40,000 travellers were stranded, some of them trapped in the tunnel itself, days before Christmas. Eurostar was completely unprepared, failed to communicate properly and left its passengers bewildered, frustrated and angry.[3]

Yet at its fingertips it had a medium it could have used to keep people informed in real time. When you're stuck in a freezing railway station, perhaps with tired children, wondering if you are ever going to get home for Christmas, all you want is to know what's going on. At the time Eurostar's social media presence was one isolated promotional campaign offering short breaks, run by an external agency.

Meanwhile, Eurostar passengers turned to social media themselves to vent their fury. One said: 'Shocked at how unprepared and uncommunicative Eurostar was. Eurostar failed to communicate with passengers and social media told the truth and got it to mainstream media fast.'

The result – a severely damaged reputation for Eurostar.

Contrast Eurostar's experience with the reaction of British Airways, other European airlines and air traffic authorities when global air travel was severely disrupted by the Icelandic volcanic ash cloud in April 2010.

Airlines used #ashcloud with their official Twitter updates and provided travellers with consistent and useful information. They managed to keep their reputations intact, despite the situation being one that they could not solve. Social media came to the fore again when stranded travellers used #getmehome and complete strangers were offering each other lifts, places to stay and other assistance, creating a brand new sector in social travel.

While the Eurostar and BA examples focus on what a company should or could communicate in different instances, there are more and more stories of individual employees responding to customer comment. In one example, Jess Greenwood from Contagious tweeted about the awful music in the Air New Zealand airport lounge where she was waiting, only to be asked over the PA system seconds later what it was she would like to hear.

The above examples demonstrate the ability of social media to create a win for everyone: the employee, who feels much more engaged, the consumer, who sees a more responsive company, and the company, which in turn benefits from both of these in terms of employee satisfaction and retention and better business performance.

4 From buying attention to earning it

In the twentieth century of Don Draper's *Mad Men*, television was still relatively novel, TV audiences captive and an entire media industry focused on buying people's attention.

Today you can still buy media, but you can no longer buy attention. You have to earn it.

No one is quite sure who first coined the now commonly used terminology 'bought, owned and earned media'. Nokia was certainly an early pioneer in the space, but what we do know is that it has become incredibly important for today's brand.

And the successful Social Brand focuses much more on earned than bought media. Earned media happens when consumers become the channel. In order for that to occur, the starting point is a powerful and engaging creative idea. The Evian Roller Babies case is just one great illustration of the power of earned versus bought media and shows how it is possible to engage consumers and achieve a level of exposure that would not have been affordable in the old media world.

At the end of 2009, *Time* magazine named the Evian Roller Babies film as their Ad of the Year – despite the fact that it had never been aired on television in the USA. It was the enormous earned media generated through YouTube, Facebook and other social platforms – with over 140 m downloads in total – that led to it being chosen as the best TV commercial of the year. But in a wonderful example of the new world, where the tail wags the dog, the massive success of the film in social media led to Havas' client Evian putting it on air as a TV commercial in mid-2010.

Similarly, the very successful award-winning campaign for Dos Equis, 'The Most Interesting Man in the World' – which in the interest of disclosure is another campaign created by Euro RSCG – also demonstrates brilliantly the power of engaging rather than interrupting consumers. While Dos Equis remains, by global standards, a small local beer brand, it is now the number-one beer page in the world on Facebook, with over a million fans. It is also the number-one page on Facebook across any alcohol category or brand. A powerful compelling idea has not only 'earned' enormous amounts of media but has also created a community of loyal fans suggesting and inputting lines and stories for what the 'Most Interesting Man in the World' may do next. All while winning the advertising effectiveness award for driving double-digit sales growth every year for the past five years.

Another great example of an ingenious idea delivering major global 'earned media' comes from Tourism Queensland from Australia. Tourism Queensland was faced with the problem that many holiday spots have: how do you stand out in a sector where there are a million pictures of beautiful beaches?

The idea of creating a job, a real job, as a caretaker on paradise location Hamilton Island and framing it as 'the best job in the world' was the inspirational solution they came up with. The campaign began with worldwide 'situations vacant' classified ads and exploded around the world. It was picked up by mainstream media, TV channels and countless newspapers, creating extraordinary momentum globally. It attracted 35,000 hopeful applicants, who uploaded videos saying why they should get the job, and even spawned a BBC documentary documenting how Ben Southall of Petersfield finally landed the job.

Tourism Queensland claims it generated £49 million of equivalent advertising space and it created awareness, attention and interest on a much broader scale than any paid-for campaign could have achieved. It shows a brilliant understanding of Social Creativity™ and how to generate earned media.

5 From 'talking at' to 'listening to'

While generating earned media is often about sending a message out, the power of social media for receiving messages should not be underestimated. One of my early bosses said to me, when advising me on how to be a good account manager: 'David, you have two ears and one mouth and you should use them in that proportion.' I have probably failed to follow that advice at too many points in my career, but if it is great advice for a career, it is even better advice for the social media world.

> the Social Brand understands it is critical to move away from talking *at* consumers and instead to really listen *to* them

For those who are nervous about how to act and engage with social media, something everyone can do is listening. It's free, easy and without risk. The Social Brand understands it is critical to move away from talking *at* consumers and instead to really listen *to* them.

One company that understands that very well is Japanese clothing retailer Uniqlo. When it redesigned its website, it first reached out to customers saying it was going to be doing this and asked for their input and feedback. This was then taken on board and integrated into the final redesign. When consumers returned to the new site they were greeted with a message saying: 'You told us, we listened, here is the new website, please tell us what you think.'

Uniqlo not only listened to consumers; it also told them it was listening and what action it was going to take. And that action was visible. This is crucial because there is no point in listening if you do not show you are hearing what is being said and doing something about it.

Uniqlo extended this smart listening to a very clever Twitter promotion that it ran just ahead of a relaunch of its e-commerce site. The basic idea was that the more people tweeted about a certain product, the lower the price of it became. Relying solely on social media for the word to be spread, the campaign was a huge success.

There are many other examples. On a small scale, Virgin America showed enormous listening skills and speed of response in having the flight attendants serve a drink to a passenger who had tweeted that he was still waiting for his pre-takeoff drink – and then equal smarts as this trend spread among passengers – they would be greeted with a simple reply that the fastest way to get one was by pushing the call button on the plane. On a larger scale, IBM is a social media pioneer and another company that really understands the importance of listening. With IBM, Euro RSCG created a programme that aggregates everything that is written about the company on any social media platform, anywhere in the world, and brings it in to one place as a real-time feed. It not only allows technologically enhanced listening – a hearing aid for the social media world – but it also allows that to be analysed and acted upon in real time.

Kodak has been a real social media pioneer, and in another tangible example of listening it appointed a chief listening officer, who oversees the monitoring of conversations across social media and the action taken as a result. If a camera user is having difficulties, Kodak will tweet and ask how it can help. In 2008, Kodak appointed a chief blogger as the voice of Kodak online and has amassed significant support. This is part of an ongoing conversation Kodak is having with its customers, which allows it to understand what they really want and to act accordingly. Do you have a chief listening officer? Or at least someone who is carrying out that function? If not, it might be time to get one and follow the advice of my first boss.

6 From controlling to collaborating

Marketing used to be all about control. Our focus was on policing brands, like gatekeepers, ensuring rigorous and ruthless adherence to what the centre had deemed the brand guidelines. And this was especially true as brands extended their reach and became global. In today's world, I would argue that the best marketers will be those who collaborate the most, not those who control the most.

It is now much more important to create content that people want to pass around and share, than to create content that you control.

One of the hardest things for marketers to accept is that they have less and less capacity to control a brand and they should open their doors and let people in. But that's the way the world is heading.

The potential benefits are enormous, and genuinely collaborating can provide spaces for a brand to create a really meaningful relationship with consumers, allowing them to feel a sense of ownership and involvement that money can't buy.

> genuinely collaborating can provide spaces for a brand to create a really meaningful relationship with consumers, allowing them to feel a sense of ownership and involvement

Pepsi is a company that has pioneered many examples of collaboration across its various brands, and a large number of its Super Bowl spots each year are created by consumers. With its Mountain Dew brand it gets consumers involved in every conceivable way: determining new flavours, voting on product names, colours and packaging. Consumers play a role in creating TV ads and have had input into media planning and buying. In 2010, Mountain Dew even turned over the choice of which marketing agency should work on its product launches by asking agencies and production companies to submit 12-second clips pitching their ideas for three brand extensions. Four thousand of the brand's most active fans, referred to as 'Dew Labs members', were asked to vote for their favourites. The brand has given this high level of consumer engagement the snappy title 'Dewmocracy'.

Furniture retailer Ikea ran a brilliantly simple campaign that both leveraged consumer involvement and used social media in an innovative way. Ikea uploaded all of the pages from its catalogue to a Facebook page. People could then 'tag' themselves on a particular item of furniture in one of the pictures. The first person who tagged themselves won that item of furniture. It was a great example of a collaborative promotion and a very fast way of building a major database.

In an example of life mirroring art, London's Victoria and Albert Museum promoted an exhibition of digital and interactive art by collaborating with potential museum visitors. One of the exhibiting artists created a piece of open-source artwork that was posted on relevant sites online, where users were able to play with the artwork, create new versions and record the results in an online gallery. The material, or as the clever pun described it 'user-renovated content', was then used to market the exhibition in digital outdoor advertising sites and on the London Underground – a clever idea that spoke directly to the target audience, involving them in the very nature of the exhibition.

There are numerous examples of collaborative marketing and we will look at some additional ones in Chapter 5. However, the critical thing is to understand the difference between collaboration and delegation. Crowd-sourcing content is not an idea in itself, or a substitute for an idea; it is just a way of getting to a great idea. Editorial control is critical. In fact, in a world where we can now generate thousands and thousands of ideas, the editor is king.

7 From local to global

Technology and social media have dramatically shrunk the world and made people realise that we are all connected, we are global citizens genuinely impacted and affected by global events. National boundaries are less and less important. This is equally true for brands.

Whether a brand is deliberately social or not, it is a fact today that there is no such thing as a local brand that can truly be contained locally. A case in point is McDonald's experience, when it launched a TV campaign in France based on its 'Come as You Are' brand strategy. 'Come as You Are' was designed to show that everyone is welcome at McDonald's, whatever their age, nationality, gender or sexuality. The ad shows a gay teenager meeting his father, who doesn't know he is gay, for a meal in McDonald's. This was a first for McDonald's in any market.

After the ad broke on TV, it immediately spilled beyond its French borders and became a YouTube sensation. Almost overnight it received more than 2.5 million views. The ad gained major coverage in the USA on the various television news programmes and sparked widespread debate as to whether McDonald's could run a similar ad there. Some of the less 'open' media were less than positive about it, with one commentator suggesting that McDonald's would soon be running ads featuring Al-Qaeda and saying that they were welcome at McDonald's too.

While this comment says more about the prejudiced commentator than it does about McDonald's, it also demonstrates very clearly that we live in an interconnected world where it is not possible to put boundaries on where content does or doesn't go.

8 From who to where

If the focus of marketing used to be all about the 'who' we were targeting, then we are now entering an era in which the 'where' we are targeting them is going to become more and more important. And here I mean their exact physical location rather than which country they are in.

The next phase of the revolution in digital communications is going to be around location-based services and geo-positioning. According to the Internet Advertising Bureau, 85% of all search enquiries are location-based, and the ability to combine search with location and product or service delivery to consumers has unbelievable potential.

To date, we have had on the one hand the virtual world of digital – with its cool, sexy and exciting image, but on the whole very little in the way of actual sales – and on the other hand the old world of traditional bricks and mortar that was often seen as 'boring' but that had the major benefit of billions of dollars of sales. With the possible exception of Amazon, the connection between digital hype and tangible sales delivery has not really happened before. In the next generation, the two will come together.

Facebook, Twitter, Foursquare, Gowalla, Shopkick – these are just some of the apps and platforms that are increasingly linking sociability with location. The Gap promotion with Facebook on 5 November 2010, where 10,000 pairs of jeans were given away to the first people to check in at a Gap store on Facebook Places, was a massive success, compelling Gap to give a 40% discount on another item to the disappointed many who got there too late. Other early examples include Starbucks 'Barista' badges or free Frappucinos for people checking in on Foursquare or Domino's UK nationwide Foursquare promotion that rewarded 'mayors' with free pizza once a week.

While these are interesting examples, we are only just starting to scratch the surface of the potential for combining location, search and retail offers. Being able to know instantly where the best deal is available for something based on where you are standing at a precise moment, with the added potential to allow retailers to enter into a bidding war for your business, overlaid with the power of Groupon-style community buying – and it's easy to imagine that the potential is as unbelievable as the way it will change retail. Imagine what the location-based, collective power on the scale of Facebook could achieve when brought to bear on purchasing.

We will see more and more examples, like Brightkite, which is incorporating augmented reality into its platform, allowing people to watch videos explaining a product – no longer will we need to wait for an assistant to come and help. We will see live real-time discounts and offers in supermarkets, not based on what you have purchased as you check out but based on what you are buying as you walk around the supermarket.

I truly think the explosion in location-based services will be the next great phase of growth in the digital revolution.

And that moving forward we now need to increasingly ask not only who are we targeting, but also where are we targeting them?

9 From discrete targeting to open access

Companies used to be able to target different audiences in different channels, often with different messages. As an extreme example, they could announce record profits to their shareholders, while explaining to consumers the need for fees to go up and to their employees the fact that there would be no pay increases.

Social media has put an end to that. Everyone has open access to everything. In real time. Tweets and posts are read by employees, shareholders, customers and the media alike.

An interesting example of this is the *Time* journalist whose Hotmail account was hacked, which in turn led to him being locked out of his inbox. After emailing Hotmail's customer service department and receiving an automated response and nothing further for three days, he vented his dissatisfaction on Twitter, tagging the message '@Microsoft' so that anyone searching for tweets about the company would see it. As he describes, 'Within 34 minutes, the 75-hour silence was broken. A Hotmail program manager contacted me via Facebook. Half an hour later, I was logged into my inbox.'

Why did this happen? Because while a customer service department email or letter is read only by that department, the tweet is read by the CEO and management team of the company, by the company's customers and consumers, by its shareholders, by the media – in simple terms, by the whole world – which puts a little bit of pressure on the employees of the customer service department to fix the problem a little quicker than in the old world.

10 From profit to purpose

If business and marketers now need to become more and more interested in where consumers are physically, consumers in turn are becoming more and more interested in where businesses are in their plans to become more socially responsible. There are massive shifts taking place as the social consumer demands that business become more socially responsible. As previously mentioned, in a global study, 86% of consumers said that they believe companies need to stand for more than just profit. Consumers want to buy from and do business with brands that share their values and beliefs.

And they will punish those businesses they view as irresponsible.

Pepsi's Refresh project is an interesting example of a brand standing for more than just profit and creating a platform that has social benefits. The company raised a few eyebrows in 2010 by investing $20 million in the Refresh project instead of purchasing the high-profile Super Bowl television spots that it had done for the previous 23 years.

The Pepsi Refresh website asks people to nominate and vote on community projects, and thousands of local initiatives will be sponsored with grants ranging from $5000 to $250,000. It's a simple mechanism – anyone can put forward ideas and PepsiCo funds those that are selected.

It gives away $1.3 million every month, which sounds like a lot of money, but given the amount of earned media, not to mention goodwill it has generated, it is relatively small when viewed in the context of PepsiCo's overall marketing spend.

We saw in the first chapter how the likes of Patagonia, GE, Walmart, Marks & Spencer and Unilever have also set out a purpose above and beyond profit for their businesses and brands. For my own business, the creation of One Young World – a not-for-profit and global movement to give the brilliant young people of the world a platform to effect positive change – was also just that. My attempt to show that we too have a purpose beyond profit.

A new generation of marketers understands that purpose is incredibly important to consumers and that in the future there will be no profit without it. Those brands that embrace this new honest and responsible world have an exciting future ahead of them. Those that don't can live in denial, but in the end they will go the way of the tobacco brands, whose reality caught up with their image in ways that were beyond their control.

CASE STUDY

Gatorade

Gatorade used authenticity as a platform for its Replay campaign. The brand reunited two former high-school football teams that, when the fierce rivals last met in 1993, had played a hotly contested match that ended in a draw – a 'sister-kisser' as one TV commentator named it. Fifteen years on, the players had replaced sport and exercise with family, career and other commitments and they were not in the kind of shape they once had been.

The players were followed for three months as they underwent training for the big rematch, the Gatorade Replay. In the process the 30-somethings made dramatic improvements to their health, with many losing more than 25lbs. One lost 57lbs and was able to come off blood pressure medication, according to Gatorade.

Source: Photograph by Steve Boyle, courtesy of Gatorade

Documentary footage was aired online and the match itself screened on Fox Sports Net.

'Replay' then became a documentary television series that was broadcast to 90 million households. Gatorade says the Replay campaign generated $3,415,255 worth of earned media and delivered a 14,000% return on investment. Sales of Gatorade in the region rose significantly and the brand has been inundated with requests from people to be selected for subsequent Replays. The most recent features basketball teams from high schools in Chicago, in a rematch of a controversial 2000 playoff game that was decided at the buzzer.

It's an example of a brand that really understands the new open world. It's absolutely authentic. It's a big content-based idea rather than a one-off advertising execution. It's a social vehicle that has health and wellness at its core. Overall it perfectly fits the Social Business Idea™ concept laid out in Chapter 6.

Brilliant ideas

The new world for the Social Brand is full of exciting possibilities as well as challenges. Marketing has been dramatically changed, by everything from the growing power of the consumer, to the disappearance of geography, to the loss of control and the need to be much more open.

I have outlined ten things that I think are substantial changes for today's Social Brand. However, one thing that hasn't changed is the power of and need for brilliant ideas. One of marketing's key roles has always been and will continue to be the creation of powerful ideas that engage consumers.

From the Evian Roller Babies to Pepsi Refresh, from Domino's Pizza to Gatorade, from Uniqlo's tweet promotion and Ikea's furniture tagging – social creativity powers the Social Brand. And those marketers who understand and leverage this power will succeed, whatever new channels and challenges appear.

Summary: the new rules for the Social Brand

▌ In the world of radical transparency, the scope for a gap between image and reality has disappeared.

▌ The old world of marketing was linear; the new one is a square where prosumers and employees can be an incredibly powerful positive or negative force for a brand.

▌ Attention can no longer be bought; it must be earned.

▌ The best companies use social media to listen to consumers, but they make sure they show they are listening and act.

▌ The best marketers will be those who collaborate and share the most, not those who control the most.

▌ 'Where' will be word of the next decade as location-based services explode.

▌ Content now travels globally; there are no boundaries on where content does or doesn't go.

▌ The new consumer wants profit with a purpose: you must do well and good.

▌ The one thing that has not changed is the power of brilliant ideas.

References

1 Euro RSCG Worldwide, *The Future of the Corporate Brand* (2008), New York, Market Probe International.

2 Havas, *Social Business Study* (2010), New York, Market Probe International.

3 http://www.telegraph.co.uk/topics/weather/6851657/ Thousands-stranded-by-Eurostar-as-chief-executive-cannot-guarantee-when-service-will-resume.html

3

Leadership in a world of radical transparency

Good leaders should also be good followers; if they cannot then we must teach them.

Kofi Annan

You can't opt out

I was recently party to a conversation where one business leader was explaining to another how social media wouldn't impact their business. To me, this was like going back in time and listening to someone saying: 'We won't be using telephones at our company' or 'This internet thing isn't relevant to our business; it won't affect us.'

While these statements may appear ridiculous today, there was a time when that's what many of the then successful business leaders were saying. And it's what many leaders are still saying today about social media.

Now, the very fact that you are reading this means it's unlikely that you are one of them. But for those who think this social media 'thing' won't affect them, it's time to think again.

Social media is here to stay, and with it both the amazing challenges and opportunities that it presents for businesses and leaders. In this new open world, disgruntled employees and consumers have a tremendous voice. Private conversations become public at the post of a tweet.

There is an ever-increasing overlap between public and private lives, with substantial consequences on relations between bosses and employees. This also affects HR policies, with the dramatic increase in public information about employees, candidates and ex-employees that is now available.

If Sarbanes-Oxley (the 2002 US law enacted in the wake of accounting scandals such as Enron) was one step to ensuring business was more transparent and accountable, then social media will be a giant leap. The new world of management is all about coping with a climate that for many is as exciting as it is scary.

The ability of people today to find out so much about companies and individuals makes it very hard to say one thing and do another. The world for leaders has dramatically changed. Everything is now completely open; it's an always-on world with no separation between public and private or between internal and external.

Social media will make business better

This transparent new world might sound daunting but the great thing about it is that it will make the business better: more authentic and more honest. After the greed-driven financial crisis with its Madoffs and Lehman Brothers, that can only be a good thing.

> the most successful companies of the future will be those whose leaders make sure their internal reality matches their external appearance

The most successful companies of the future will be those whose leaders make sure their internal reality matches their external appearance and that put doing the right thing at the core of the business. Consumers insistent that business does its part to improve the world are not totally unrealistic; nor do they expect miracles to be performed overnight. What they want to see from business leaders is commitment, effort, progress and honesty about that progress.

> Put simply, corporate social responsibility helps us to attract shoppers to our stores, recruit and retain the best people, form better partnerships with our suppliers and create greater value for our shareholders.
>
> Paul Myners, former chairman of Marks & Spencer

As a moral compass for decision-making, we used to say that you should run your business imagining that every decision you made was being printed as the headline on the front page of a newspaper and ask yourself how comfortable you would feel about that.

In today's world, social media is that moral compass, but it is actually no longer a theoretical exercise. You will be reading about your decisions in social media on a weekly, daily, hourly or even minute-by-minute basis.

Reputations take years to build but can now be destroyed in seconds. And we have seen numerous cases of this happening – from the inevitable consequences of BP-style corner-cutting to the careless comment or tweet of a CEO or founder – as in the case of Kenneth Cole's inappropriate tweets around Egypt, which I describe later.

It isn't just social media that has dramatically changed the operating environment for today's business leader. The social consumer, as we discussed in Chapter 1, is looking for businesses and leaders to be much more socially responsible and is forcing it in a better direction. The twenty-first-century manager must align this consumer demand with the sometimes conflicting views of other significant stakeholders.

Social responsibility and sustainability are both inherently a mid- to long-term proposition, with impacts sometimes taking years to be seen. For the financial markets, long term is often viewed as a year, mid term as this quarter and short term as this week.

Business leaders are increasingly caught in the middle of a tug of war between consumers pushing the business to be more socially responsible on the one hand, and the board and shareholders pushing for greater and greater returns at any cost on the other hand.

This is compounded by the fact that many boards today are still composed of people who grew up in a different era with different values. I have had several conversations with progressive CEOs who have added sustainability to the bonus criteria of their key direct reports, but whose board had little or no interest in making it part of their own CEO compensation.

Further complexity is added by the fact that several of the quick wins that do have an immediate impact on the business are one-offs. Major progress on reducing transport and fuel costs or on reducing packaging tends to have a significant impact in year one, but the benefit of that is lost after a year when the new comparatives kick in.

Finally, there are challenges of marrying social responsibility with competition. Even when a leader has a free hand to implement change to create a more sustainable business, drive efficiencies, cut down on waste and so on, the most efficient thing to do might be to replace people with technology or machines. If you do this, it clearly has a human cost and could hardly be described as being socially responsible. If you don't do it, the negative impact on the business may be so great that many more people lose their jobs or the business might not even survive.

There is no easy answer, and the new social management world presents the social boss with many of these unenviable dilemmas.

Doing good and doing well

Despite these challenges, we are seeing a new breed of socially responsible CEOs who are leading their companies on the path to being better businesses. Some, who are in positions of great power and responsibility, really understand the social, commercial and environmental shifts that are happening. They are spearheading the move to doing business better from within the corporate sector – leading from the front. These include Paul Polman at Unilever, Jeff Immelt at GE, Mike Duke at Walmart, Jeff Swartz at Timberland, Tex Gunning at Dulux, Indra Nooyi at PepsiCo and many more I could name.

What they generally have in common is the following:

▌ They have made social responsibility core to their business strategy rather than leaving it in a silo or treating it as a marketing tactic.

▌ They make very apparent that they have done this in order to both do good and do well.

▌ They are united by a belief that you can both do well and feel better about yourself and your company, that you can deliver better corporate performance and be a better corporate citizen.

It is important we understand that saving money and saving the environment need *not* be mutually exclusive.

Reckitt Benckiser, outgoing global CEO, Bart Becht

Unilever CEO Paul Polman, as mentioned in Chapter 1, surprised many in 2010 by committing the company to halving its environmental impact while aiming to double its sales over the subsequent ten years. He sent further ripples of surprise through the City when he announced in November 2010 how these targets were going to be reached and some detail of what changes were going to be implemented. He said that they were a long-term value-creation model and more or less told short-term investors that their money was not wanted at Unilever. This kind of leadership is committed and fearless because, despite doing the right thing, Unilever's share price fell when he made this announcement.

When Polman, a One Young World Counsellor, made these commitments, it was a very clear signal for the entire company and all its stakeholders of just how serious he was about this subject. He said: 'It is the right way to do business'. Polman has since changed Unilever's financial reporting practice: it will no longer publish full earnings statements quarterly but instead will switch to a six-monthly cycle and issue a short trading statement in the intervening quarters (Qs 1 and 3) in an effort to move investors away from judging the company on a 90-day basis.

It is only through the responsible actions of companies of this scale that social responsibility will become a mainstream philosophy rather than a siloed activity or marketing tactic. But it is not easy; there will be resistance and it requires steadfast leadership.

Sustainability is not optional. This is an opportunity to step out in leadership.

Mike Duke, CEO, Walmart

How not to do it #fail

One CEO we couldn't accuse of leading his business on a better path is the now dislodged BP CEO Tony Hayward. While he can't be used as a great example of a new age CEO whom we should try to emulate, he can provide a lesson about how to manage in the new social world.

When the Deepwater Horizon oil rig blew up in the Gulf of Mexico, Hayward was possibly hoping it would all just go away. To make matters worse, he supplied endless ammunition for onlookers to berate him. Here is just a small selection of gaffes from the hapless Mr Hayward, who turned himself into the world's favourite whipping boy.

'There's no one who wants this thing over more than I do; I'd like my life back.' Even though this much-repeated quote is taken slightly out of context, it was unbelievably ill-considered given the 11 people who had lost their lives in the explosion.

After seven oil-spill clean-up workers were hospitalised for sickness, dizziness and nausea, which, according to doctors, were probably caused by chemical irritation and dehydration from working in oppressive heat, Hayward said: 'I am sure they were genuinely ill, but whether it was anything to do with dispersants and oil, whether it was food poisoning or some other reason for them being ill ...'

And even though he said it only a few days after the spill occurred, 'I think the environmental impact of this disaster is likely to have been very, very modest' was not exactly what his head of PR would have been hoping for.

Be fast, be authentic, be transparent

All major companies will face a crisis at some point – maybe not of the epic proportions BP faced, but some crisis is unavoidable. The key thing is to be prepared for it.

When the crisis happens, old-world corporate communications systems, which seek to batten down the hatches and issue 'safe' impersonal statements, at their own pace, will simply no longer do. It's about being fast, authentic and transparent. Or else people will feel, as they did with BP, that the company and the people behind it just do not care.

> if you say something you must consider that it will probably be taken out of context, predictions will come back to haunt you and your actions will be scrutinised

As a boss, if you say something you must consider that it will probably be taken out of context, predictions will come back to haunt you and, as well as your words, your actions will be scrutinised – Hayward discovered this when he had sufficient lack of foresight to go sailing with his son on the shining waters around the Isle of Wight while the Gulf of Mexico was choking on black sludge. It was totally irrelevant that it was his first day off in months and that he hadn't seen his son for a lengthy period. No one cared. All people saw were pictures of him enjoying a day out near a pristine beach. He was accused of abandoning his post, and the location served only to rub salt in the wound.

I witnessed a small example from the oil industry that demonstrated that being transparent, open and honest does

work. We organised an event in London in 2010 all about the
future of the caring corporation. One of the guest speakers was
James Smith, the UK chairman of Shell. The event was being
live-streamed on the internet. It was taking place the week of
the BP oil spill. I said to my team that we could forget Smith's
attendance as his PR people would never let him come and
speak at a live-streamed event, on socially responsible business,
the week of Deepwater Horizon. Smith did, however, attend.
He gave a short presentation and then took about 30 minutes
of very hostile and angry questioning. He answered every
question head-on, explained what the issues and problems
were and what they were trying to do about it. He was open
and honest and genuine. And at the end of the session we
all sat there thinking that this was nowhere near as simple as
it seemed and we had an enhanced respect for Smith and a
greater understanding of the complexity of the task facing Shell.

People now demand transparency. Toyota CEO Akio
Toyoda made the mistake of trying to keep a lid on the
safety problems that emerged with some vehicles in late
2009. Toyota was accused of failing to inform the proper
authorities of the issues and, as the situation unfolded, with
recall after recall, the company looked like it was trying to
conceal issues that might have an impact on people's safety.
In the early days of the recalls, Toyoda himself was invisible
and earned the nickname 'No-Show Akio'.

The ill-feeling was fuelled by the US media, which probably
relished the chance to attack the Japanese car industry.
Nevertheless, it demonstrates that among the biggest
mistakes people can make is to believe they can control an
issue or that they've got time. In the social media world, you
need to assume that little issues will become major global
crises instantaneously.

A contrasting and recent example of good leadership came
from Sidney Toledano, president of Christian Dior Couture.

In another era, no one would have known about star designer John Galliano's anti-Semitic rant. But in the new world, what is said in a late-night private drunken rant can go around the world and be seen by thousands of people in a matter of seconds. This was the case for Galliano when a video surfaced showing him declaring his love for Hitler. It is hard to imagine a more damaging statement. Toledano's response was immediate and unequivocal: Galliano was out, no matter how brilliant a designer; Dior's policy towards anti-Semitism was 'zero tolerance'. Toledano then made a sombre, dignified but short speech at Dior's Paris show, which coincidentally took place only a few days after the scandal blew up. He denounced Galliano's outburst, firmly restated the company's values, and, with these acts of decisive leadership, extinguished the crisis.

Be prepared – social media is always on the record

One of the further challenges for leaders today is that it has become impossible to say different things to different audiences. Everything you say will be seen, read and heard by all of your audiences.

Where once it was possible to discretely target different audiences, today your shareholders, your employees, your consumers and the media can all see everything you say and do. We are living in an open world with free access for everybody to everything. And we all need to behave like that.

At a private dinner in July 2010, General Electric CEO Jeffrey Immelt made comments about the Chinese government that sparked a global furore and ended up appearing on the front page of the *Financial Times* – Immelt's explanation that his comments were made in private and taken out of context was true, but to no avail. Anything you say can now be broadcast globally to everybody and taken totally out of context.

I experienced a minor version of this myself when I was named as the CEO of Havas. A journalist from *Advertising Age* wrote an article on my nomination. In order to make the point that I was of a different generation from my peers running the other holding companies and that I was a digitally savvy CEO, the journalist shared some of my recent Facebook posts. These included a post from the TED conference – 'Sitting 5 seats down from Cameron Diaz at TED – I wish she'd stop staring at me :)' – and another one on landing after one too many flights: 'The joys of jetlag, 2am here and so wide awake there's no chance of sleeping, yet tomorrow at 7am when the alarm goes off I will want to die … #fuckihatetravelling'. While hardly likely to cause an international furore on the scale of Immelt's, I felt pretty uncomfortable about the article for a day or so – having been brought up by my parents not to swear. And it was a good reminder for me of my own point that personal and private lives are now the same. And that posts written with my friends in mind are also being seen by colleagues, clients, journalists and employees.

The other key issue is that digital doesn't die. And things said years ago can be found easily and can come back to haunt you. Stuart McLennan, a UK Labour Party election candidate, was forced to resign over posts he had made on Twitter, some of them when he was still a student. What might have been funny banter among college mates became a lot less funny a year later when he was standing for Parliament. 'In the queue at the Post Office. Absolutely massive. Must be pension day. Bloody coffin dodgers' is not so amusing when the 'coffin dodgers' have become elderly voters. The same goes for 'Johnnie Walker Red Label is so awful they can't sell it in Scotland', when the whisky industry is a major employer in one's potential constituency. In digital and social media, comments can live forever.

People are people and we will continue to make errors and gaffes. Probably the most important advice is that if you make a mistake, you need to own up to it straight away. Clothes and shoe designer Kenneth Cole made an extremely inappropriate tweet, suggesting the unrest in Egypt was due to people trying to get their hands on his new spring fashion line. This sparked an immediate furious reaction initially on Twitter and then across all of the main news media. But Cole, to his credit, immediately scotched speculation that an employee had been responsible, admitted he had done it himself and apologised. The world moved on.

If today you have a small, local issue, you should assume it will become massive and global, instantly. The scout's motto of 'be prepared' is great advice for today's business leader. You should assume you have got no time to formulate plans of how to address issues after they arise. Anticipate what issues may arise and plan how you will respond when they do. And if something occurs that you weren't expecting, try to pre-empt things. Say something yourself first. At least the conversation can then begin on your terms and you will get credit for being open and honest.

The speed and response of a company and its employees are extremely important. Sometimes employees can be reluctant to engage in social media on behalf of their employers. This is partly because they are often uncertain about what they should and shouldn't say and what might happen if they say the wrong thing. So no one responds – this is the worst possible thing to allow to happen. If you move too slowly, and this can mean making even the slightest hesitation, then you allow scope for things to spiral out of all proportion, often quite needlessly.

Social media exposes true corporate culture

For so long, Apple has been held up as the shining example of all that is brilliant in business and marketing, but with the launch of the iPhone 4 in June 2010 the company was surprisingly inept when it came to social media. This was not about the product quality problems but about how Apple responded to them. From failing to comment on the issue or respond to consumer complaints, to bizarre explanations, to reportedly deleting negative posts from its tech support forums, Apple did the exact opposite of what it should have done.

A rapid response, acknowledging the issue and explaining what it was doing about it, would have kept everyone happy and kept several billion dollars more on the company's market cap. We all love Apple so much that we would let it get away with a great deal more than any other brand.

After all, in my experience, Apple's product quality has never totally matched its design quality. I think I went through four iPods in the early years, and my wife's first iPhone didn't ring (or at least that's what she told me). We know that if we sign up for their latest launch, we're likely to have a few teething problems – although that risk is totally overshadowed by the enormous sense of smugness we have when we are the first to place the new iThing on the restaurant table.

The antisocial boss

So why did Apple get it so wrong? After all, it is so brilliant at the PR and stage management around product launches. The answer, I think, comes from the top. Steve Jobs was a genius. To revolutionise one industry is incredible. There is no adequate word to describe revolutionising four industries (computing, mobile communications, music and film). It's highly unlikely that we will ever see his like again.

But Jobs was also criticised for being highly autocratic. And when you are like that, people don't feel empowered to respond quickly, as they need to today, to issues such as this. They wait for permission. So PR departments say things like 'no comment'. Today, there is no longer such a thing as 'no comment'.

Decide who within the company is empowered to respond. Some place the task of reacting and responding to comment in social media within PR, but in reality it cuts across everything – customer service, quality control, distribution, investor relations, marketing and so on – and therefore in my view a broader focus is probably needed – but wherever it lives, the key is to ensure that someone is empowered to react and respond.

Give authority to staff, define who deals with what and support them. If employees are allowed and encouraged to experiment with platforms, backed when they make instant decisions and speak publicly for an organisation, then the corollary is that they will come up with ideas as to how to improve the consumers' interface with the company and help build systems that improve the customers' experience and the employees' role.

Giving someone carte blanche to respond on behalf of a corporation goes against all the traditional rules of corporate crisis management, but the world has changed and corporations have to change the way they communicate too.

The social media world closes the gap between a company's external image and its internal reality. In the wake of its iPhone 4 product quality issues, Apple users perhaps saw that the reality of Apple wasn't quite as shiny as its image. Being user-friendly is something Apple understands in the creation of its wonderful products, but apparently not so well in its corporate culture.

Be worried

There are enormous potential negatives that come alongside the enormous positives of social media. It's right to be worried about what your employees are doing and saying in social media. But when disaster does happen, it is then about how you react.

The notorious example of a company being humiliated by its own employees on social media is the YouTube video uploaded by staff from a North Carolina Domino's Pizza who filmed themselves doing fairly unappetising things to food. The video had a million views in 48 hours and 10 million views within 72 hours. Brand perception plummeted and the incident was a trending topic on Twitter for 56 hours, an incredibly long time for that channel. It also became the major news item across all of the main TV news programmes. Within a week, Domino's share price had dropped 7%. In just a few short days a YouTube video had done horrendous damage to the business.

The workers were fired and faced criminal charges, though they insisted that the food was never served to any customers and it was just a prank. It is interesting to note that the act of uploading a video did not contravene any company policy at that time.

This incident is the background that led up to the Domino's campaign in Chapter 2, and what is especially interesting is how the company reacted. It responded by positioning its entire marketing and communications strategy on transparency and turned a negative into a positive. CEO Patrick Doyle made his own YouTube video outlining exactly what the company was going to do to make sure that something like that would never happen again. A thorough review of Domino's policy then followed, which included a staff code of conduct and a plan to improve consumer engagement.

Engaging your employees

Domino's 'Pizza Turnaround' was an open campaign engaging Domino's staff too, many of whom blogged on the website to defend their work and speak on behalf of the brand, generating authentic and credible brand building.

The Domino's case is a great example of how social media allows you to motivate employees to become powerful advocates. Today, many companies are not structured in a way that allows staff to take advantage of the technology available. It goes against the grain to share control among employees. However, if steps are taken that will harness employees' creativity and sense of usefulness, it can be transformational and can provide a powerful point of differentiation between a business and its competitors.

Best Buy gets as many consumer queries and complaints as its competitors but it deals with them differently – to great effect. More than 2500 Best Buy employees, some of them customer service staff, some sales agents, some technical support staff, some service engineers, are engaged as the Twelpforce, which enables them to see what customers are saying about Best Buy on Twitter and to respond by helping customers with their queries, correcting misperceptions or even taking on board changes that the company needs to make.

They can then tweet in reply using #Twelpforce. The tweet also appears on the Twelpforce website, where all tweets are aggregated so everybody can see who is saying what in response to questions and problems.

This is not replacing customer service; it is enhancing it in a new way. It is creatively using the technology that's available and bringing the Best Buy in-store customer experience, with its knowledgeable and helpful staff, to an online, real-time environment.

But full disclosure is important too. It's important to explain to your employees that while being positive about the company or brand is a good thing, it needs to be done in a transparent and honest way. A very enthusiastic Honda employee joined in with a debate on a Facebook page about a new family SUV, the Honda Accord Crosstour. Amid waves of criticism, a lone poster called Eddie OKubo appeared extolling the virtues of this marvellous car, which he would buy 'in a heartbeat'. It took two minutes for the contributor to be outed as the product manager for Honda North America, and a serious digital lashing occured.

If employees believe in the company's values and products, they will clearly be much more predisposed to be positive advocates through social media. And for the social consumer, and especially the Millennial generation, the values of the company they work for will become more and more important. I think we will see the rise of 'employalty', where loyalty to companies will be driven less and less by financial incentives and rewards and more and more by shared values and pride in the social contribution an organisation is making. Forward-thinking companies such as Google encourage staff to take paid days off in order to take part in socially beneficial activities in the wider community. Not only will the most socially responsible businesses do better because consumers reward them and become powerful advocates for their brand and businesses, but also they will do better because the best talent will want to work for them.

According to an interesting recent survey by PricewaterhouseCoopers, graduates place a very high value on a company's CSR policies. The survey found that 71% of recent graduates would rather work for a business with strong ethical values, while an even bigger number, 76%, said they would actually consider leaving a firm because of its CSR policies – or lack of them.

To friend or not to friend, that is the question

Harnessing the power of employees using social media is one thing, but what happens when an employee asks to be your friend on Facebook?

Clearly this blurs the distinction between personal and professional lives in a fairly significant way. And it's a tricky question for those business leaders who are embarking into the social media world. My answer is that it really depends on the sector you work in. If you work in a sector where communications, technology or media are important, then there could well be important reasons to accept the request. If you are in a more traditional sector or where there is less of a business reason, I think you can feel justified in not accepting the request.

From my perspective I invariably accept employee requests as I don't believe I can call upon my company globally to embrace and lead the social media revolution and the new open and transparent world and then block and deny them access. It would be a bit like being in advertising in the 1950s and not having a TV at home. That said, it's important to then update and post knowing that it is being read by your employees or at the very least understand that they may well be watching – which as I mentioned before is something I sometimes forget.

When it comes to the boss reaching out to befriend employees, my advice would be not to do it. From an employee's perspective, there are the issues in letting their boss into their private lives, but they are exacerbated by the fact that, in general, given their age, they are likely to be leading more entertaining and colourful social lives and have more to be concerned about sharing. I personally believe that a friend request puts the employee in the difficult position of either feeling compelled to accept and then worrying about the consequences or, alternatively, feeling very awkward about how to decline without creating a workplace issue.

I think either side should feel comfortable saying, 'Thanks for the friend request but I prefer to keep my personal and professional lives separate'. More subtle ways out could be to decline a Facebook friend request but suggest following each other on Twitter, or to connect using a professional social network such as LinkedIn. Other ways might be to not reply for a few weeks and then respond with 'Thanks for your request but I don't use this very often' or to set up different accounts for professional and personal friends.

This debate also illustrates one of the major issues around social media. There is no such thing as context. We don't expect our employees to behave on a Friday night out in the same way as they would on a Monday morning in a key meeting, but in the social media world the two can sit side by side in a wall post. I therefore believe that there is an onus on the social boss to be relaxed about some of the things they may see if they end up being friends with their employees. My personal view is that HR should not look to find out more about candidates' or employees' social lives on social media. After all, we wouldn't follow someone to a bar at the weekend to see how they behave. And those of us who were lucky enough to grow up without this kind of scrutiny shouldn't try to inflict it on this generation.

Things will change and evolve as social media becomes more established and as generational shifts permeate throughout business. One of my colleagues recently recounted the response her student daughter gave, when she cautioned her about posting too many things about herself on Facebook, saying that one day they might cost her a job. Her daughter replied: 'No, Mum, because the people who will be hiring me will be much more like me than like you.' This very nicely sums up the generational divide.

And, while the older generation baulks at the idea of letting the world into their lives, the younger generation believes it's completely normal to share the most intimate details about their lives with total strangers. In my view, many of the concerns about privacy that the older generation are currently voicing will disappear as the younger generation matures and their level of openness becomes the norm.

Social media gets legal

Two recent cases on either side of the Atlantic show that social media isn't just a philosophical issue and debate; it's also a legal one. In France the Alten engineering company fired three workers when they criticised their bosses on Facebook. They did this on a Saturday night from their homes. A fourth 'so-called' friend of theirs on Facebook, in an extremely unfriendly gesture, took screen grabs of the posts and sent them to senior managers in the company, leading to the three being dismissed for smearing the company name and incitement to rebellion.

The three employees took the case to a tribunal, claiming that the comments were made in private, but the tribunal turned down their appeal. It was the first time in France that Facebook remarks were used to fire someone, and this clearly sets an interesting and complicated precedent.

In the USA a similar case went in the opposite direction. The National Labor Relations Board ordered American Medical Response of Connecticut to reinstate Dawnmarie Souza after she was fired for criticising her boss on Facebook, judging that comments on Facebook were equivalent to chatting at the coffee machine and were therefore everybody's right.

Some of her posts were very direct and critical and designed to be entertaining, one reported example being: 'Love how the company allows a 17 to become a supervisor.' The term '17' is how the company describes a psychiatric patient. The board's acting general counsel, Lafe Solomon, said: 'This is a fairly straightforward case under the National Labor Relations Act – whether it takes place on Facebook or at the water cooler, it was employees talking jointly about working conditions, in this case about their supervisor, and they have a right to do that.'

This is a first and an interesting case where a labour board has argued that workers' criticisms of their bosses or companies on a social networking site are generally a protected activity. And like the French case, it sets another, albeit diametrically opposite precedent.

Finally, a slightly more entertaining example is the case of the ten pupils who were suspended from school after using Facebook to call for protests against President Nicolas Sarkozy's pension reforms. Their punishment, however, was a nice reminder of pre-digital days – according to *Liberation*, a French newspaper, they were ordered to write a comparative analysis of European pension systems.

Having a policy is a good policy

Whether you find the above entertaining, interesting or alarming, what it clearly demonstrates is the importance not only of having a social media policy but also in reviewing it. American Medical Response of Connecticut had a policy barring employees from depicting the company 'in any way' on Facebook or other social media sites in which they post pictures of themselves. But this was ruled as being 'overly broad' and overly restrictive in limiting employees' rights to discuss working conditions among themselves.

The majority of American businesses still do not have a social media policy at the time of writing. The main reasons for not having one range from not believing social media will have an impact on business to not knowing what to include.

To mitigate the risk, it's important to establish a policy and make everyone aware of what they should and shouldn't do. That way you can help guard against some potential disasters. It's vital in preparing this policy to review with legal, HR and IT departments the risks that social media places on your specific business.

I have listed some key points to bear in mind in the box below.

Tips for formulating a company social media policy

▌ Set out the company's point of view overall – are you keen for everyone to take part, or do you view it as something you'd rather not be encouraging?

▌ Don't be too heavy-handed – a light touch is much better.

▌ Be human – appeal to employees to use their judgement and common sense.

- Remind people that standard company policies apply in social media as they do in the real world – everything from confidentiality and proprietary information to ethics, codes of conduct, harassment and so on.

- Explain the importance of the difference between personal and professional identities to ensure that personal opinions and comments aren't seen as company lines and encourage the use of disclaimers where any issues could arise.

- Transparency, honesty and authenticity are critical – ensure that any positive comments or posts about the company's products or business have full disclosure about the individual's employer.

- Be clear on what is or what is not allowed by the company – from tweeting what is said in management meetings to taking workplace videos or photos.

- Explain how the company will monitor social media use.

- Tell people whom they should contact if they have a question or are unsure about something to do with social media.

The apocryphal policy of explaining to employees 'Don't do anything you couldn't explain to your boss on a Monday morning or that you wouldn't want your grandmother to ask you about over Sunday lunch' actually makes a huge amount of sense as a guide to using social media. It's interesting that on Facebook, where people's identities are known, there is a lot less negativity and profanity than in those forums where anonymous posting and comments take place.

One question people often ask as a solution to keeping control is should social media be banned in the workplace? I would strongly advise against this. Technology has dramatically changed the working day and most people now spend a lot of time working when they are technically on their own time. My view is to be relaxed about people using social media at work; after all, we don't pay them extra for sending emails or working at 11 at night, and good employees will always deliver.

Don't seek to control, seek to create value

As leaders, we are on the whole used to controlling things to such an extent that we could almost believe it is one of the key jobs of management. But it isn't. Management's role isn't to control, it's to create value. Social media provides a number of powerful ways of creating value: from enhancing collaboration; to allowing 'listening'; to improving communication; to sharing ideas; to basically using this fast, free and ubiquitous tool to great advantage.

> the most successful leaders won't be those who try to control everything but will be those who relax and leverage this revolution to the benefit of their businesses

In fact, the most successful leaders won't be those who try to control everything but will be those who relax and leverage this revolution to the benefit of their businesses. However, the only way to truly understand this revolution is to be part of it. Tweet, blog, post, listen and interact with employees, friends, customers and the media.

There go my people, I must hurry and catch them, for I am their leader.

Gandhi

I remember sitting in my office explaining to one of our digital gurus why Twitter wouldn't work and why I wouldn't be tweeting. Three months of daily use later I had done a complete about-turn. Today it has become my number-one source of news, my way of staying in touch with trends, of following our clients' and prospects' activities, of keeping an eye on competitors, a key source of ideas and inspiration for my speeches and presentations, and a great communications vehicle with employees, potential employees and friends.

Like mine, many people's initial reactions to social media vary from thinking it is one of the most pointless things they have ever seen, to being embarrassed about sharing their thoughts and views publicly. Everyone goes through this – it's part of the social media IQ test.

Someone who has built a whole business strategy around social media is Tony Hsieh of online shoe retailer Zappos. Hsieh is a pioneer in the social media space and, along with other platforms, has used Twitter in particular to provide unparalleled service to Zappos customers. Through personal connections and encouraging his employees to be social, he has humanised the business in a way that has engendered amazing customer loyalty and advocacy. Hsieh is often held up as *the* example of a social boss, and what he has to say about his experience is revealing.

In a terrific blog that can be found on www.zappos.com, Hsieh explains how Twitter has made his company a better company. In simple terms, the discipline of tweeting regularly is making him constantly ask himself whether his actions are living up to what he is saying and to the stated company values and beliefs. This kind of honest self-appraisal will be a major component of successful businesses of the future. In 2009 Hsieh sold Zappos to Amazon for approximately $900 million.

Being a good leader

All of these new and evolving subject areas make being a leader in the social age a complex proposition. The impact of the two century-defining phenomena of social media and socially responsible business means there has probably never been a more challenging time to be a leader.

It's also a brand-new exciting world where we are all learning and the rulebook is being written. Experiment and innovate and don't be afraid to get things wrong. An added benefit for leaders in this new world is that today, having all the answers is viewed as less important than being honest and open.

Speed, transparency and authenticity are not only the rules of the game for social media; they are the rules of the game for running a modern business.

Ensure that your actions and calendar reflect your priorities and beliefs. Be aware that some of the smartest people to help you navigate this new environment are the youngest people in the company. Leading a socially responsible and sustainable business may set the progressive leader against some other stakeholders, temporarily at least, but it is important to hold firm.

Above all – lead by example. If you want your employees or consumers to feel excited and passionate about your company, then be the kind of company people get excited

> if you want your employees or consumers to feel excited and passionate about your company, then be the kind of company people get excited about working for

about working for. If you want to be seen as a decent and socially responsible company, then act in a decent and socially responsible way.

And social media will take care of the rest.

Summary: how to get social

■ Social media is here to stay; leaders can't opt out.

■ The only way to understand it is to be part of it – tweet, blog, post, listen.

■ Use and leverage social media in your business for everything, from listening to customers, employees and competitors, to engaging with key stakeholders, to sharing information, to selling.

■ Progressive leaders make it clear it is possible to do good and do well; they put CSR at the heart of business strategy rather than leaving it in a silo.

■ A key management challenge is reconciling consumers' desire for business to be more socially responsible with the often short-term mentality of the financial markets.

■ There is no longer such a thing as 'off the record' – imagine that anything you say anywhere can immediately become public.

■ Social media brings a massive overlap between the public and private lives of everyone in the company – including your own – and with it substantial consequences on boss–employee relations and HR policies.

▌ Ensure you have a social media policy.

▌ If you want employees to feel passionate about your business, be the kind of business people get excited about working for.

▌ Use the power of the Millennial employee – the pyramid has now turned upside down, and the youngest employees understand the most about the digital and social revolution we are living through.

▌ Management's role isn't to control, it's to create value.

▌ Transparency, speed and authenticity are the rules of the social media world and the rules for running a modern business.

▌ Above all, lead by example.

Plate 1: On Creativity 2.0 Panel with Bill Gates in 2007
Source: Courtesy of Corbis

Plate 2: With Kofi Annan and Bob Geldof in front of the tck tck tck ice sculpture for the launch of the Campaign for Climate Justice

Source: Courtesy of www.agencerea.com

Plate 3: With Kofi Annan and Mélanie Laurent launching 'Beds Are Burning' track in support of Campaign for Climate Justice
Source: Courtesy of Jérôme Sessini, photographer

Plate 4: David Cameron in the offices of Euro RSCG London thanking us for our work on the Conservatives' campaign 2007–2010

Source: Courtesy of Daniel Sims, photographer

Plate 5: On stage with Kofi Annan at Cannes Advertising Festival 2009 launching tck tck tck

Source: Courtesy of www.agencerea.com

Plate 6: With One Young World Co-Founder Kate Robertson and Archbishop Desmond Tutu at the start of One Young World 2011

Source: Courtesy of Martyn Hicks Photography

Plate 7: Celebrating Archbishop Tutu's 80th birthday with Bob Geldof, Kate Robertson and Kay Pratt

Source: Courtesy of Martyn Hicks Photography

Plate 8: Professor Muhammad Yunus applauds the announcement of the One Young World Social Business Fund

Source: Courtesy of Anthony Dodge, videographer

Creating good: the rise of the social entrepreneur

I find out what the world needs, then I proceed to invent it.

Thomas Edison

The leaders of large global corporations, like those mentioned in the previous chapter, are only one part of the story behind the overall move to social responsibility and sustainability. Alongside powerful business leaders reassessing their role in society and acting for the greater good are scores of people, many of them young, who have decided financial profit is not everything and are starting brand new ventures. And there are also those at the heart of the developments in technology and social media itself. I would define them all as social entrepreneurs. And the world of big business has many lessons to learn from them.

But I do believe that the leaders of large international companies not only can but *should* be included in the definition of social entrepreneurs as well. The Oxford Dictionary defines an entrepreneur as 'a person who organizes and operates a business or businesses, taking on greater than normal financial risks in order to do so'. I would argue that to take some of the biggest companies in the world and lead them down a socially responsible path, when the financial case and return for shareholders is as yet unproven, is as entrepreneurial as anything that you will see in the business world. Entrepreneurship is also not tied to small-scale business; some of the most successful entrepreneurs created the world's biggest businesses – people like the late Steve Jobs and Sir Richard Branson, along with many others.

> the key to making social responsibility mainstream is ensuring it is a sustainable and potentially profitable proposition

Big business leaders have a critical role to play and they must be encouraged to be social entrepreneurs within their own companies, because the key to making social responsibility mainstream is ensuring it is a sustainable and potentially profitable proposition.

In this chapter we look at four main types of social entrepreneur:

- Those behind businesses that were founded in or around social media, with open business models. Jimmy Wales (Wikipedia), Craig Newmark (Craigslist), Andrew Mason (Groupon) and Mark Zuckerberg (Facebook) are all good examples.

- Those in established, often huge companies, who are driving their businesses to be much more socially responsible, either from the top, such as Unilever's Paul Polman and Walmart's Mike Duke, or from within, working to convince the wider organisation.

- Those running businesses that put social responsibility at their core when created. John Replogle, former CEO of Burt's Bees, Yvon Chouinard, founder of Patagonia, Bono and Bobby Shriver, who created RED, and Anita Roddick's Body Shop all fit in this category.

- Those playing at the intersection of social media and

social responsibility. This group includes initiatives such as One, Pants to Poverty and newer entrants like Facebook founder Chris Hughes' new business Jumo, which has recently merged with GOOD and aims to connect people with causes. This group is where I believe we will see more and more examples being created over the next decade and from where I believe the next Facebook or Google may come.

Together, these four types of social entrepreneur are transforming modern business and driving social responsibility to a new level.

Social media entrepreneurs

Mark Zuckerberg, one of the richest entrepreneurs in the world, wasn't motivated by monetising Facebook. But the history books, read on whatever version of Kindle is around in 100 years, will portray him as one of the most important entrepreneurs in the revolution we are living through and Facebook as a major driver of societal change. Although, as Doug Richard amusingly commented, little did Zuckerberg know, that in his desire to get a date, he would change the world.

The industrial entrepreneurs of the second half of the twentieth century were (generally speaking) focused on financial gain; in the new world the social entrepreneurs of the twenty-first century are focused on social change. If you compare today's entrepreneurs with those from even just the previous generation, there are massive differences. People like Zuckerberg and his peers Jimmy Wales, Pierre Omidyar, (eBay), Andrew Mason and Craig Newmark place openness, sharing and collaboration at the centre of what they do, whereas their predecessors made ownership and closed business models their foundation.

Zuckerberg, for example, simply gave Facebook to everybody who wanted to join. And I would argue that if he had charged for access, Facebook would more than likely have remained a small niche network shared across some privileged Ivy League colleges. But he didn't – his is a free distribution model (for users, at least) and that is what he and his peers have in common. They scale their businesses by allowing easy, free access.

Zuckerberg is also probably the best example of the dramatic change in the importance and power of young people in today's world. Imagine explaining to people a mere decade ago that *Time* magazine's person of the year 2011 and star of the 2011 G8 meeting would be a 27-year-old – who actually only attended the G8 on the basis that he was granted a one-on-one meeting with each of the leaders of the G8 countries – and that this 27-year-old had become the youngest billionaire on the planet at the age of 24 on the back of a business he had launched when he was just 20 years old.

Groupon's founder Andrew Mason began his journey as a social entrepreneur by founding The Point, which united people around collective action and fundraising. The idea was that people should do well or do good, but only when it matters. As its website explains: 'Whether you're asking people to do something or give money, people only contribute if they think it makes a difference. On The Point, all campaigns have a "tipping point" – people *pledge* to give money or do something, but no one does a thing until the conditions are met to make contributions worthwhile. That way, you can gather all the resources needed to be successful before anyone is asked to take action', and so only when sufficient numbers of people had signed up for a cause of fundraising donation did any action occur.

From production-led to consumption-led

The Point was intended to help people congregate around issues they cared about, but it didn't take Mason long to realise that he could deploy the collective power of the group to commercial aims to get discounts from local businesses. This formed the basis of Groupon: collective bargain hunting. The potential for Groupon and similar businesses is enormous. Whether it is uniting the power of massive groups of people to drive huge cost-savings for consumers or taking advantage of location-based technology for hyper-local deals, it has the potential to change the dynamic of producer–consumer relations. And if the Industrial Revolution was a production-led revolution, then the social revolution will be a consumption-led one.

It's perhaps also not surprising as we talk about the need to do well and to do good in today's world that the inspiration for Groupon, the fastest business in history to reach $1 billion in revenue, came from a business that was designed entirely around doing good. In the twentieth century businesses set out to do well and then sometimes later focused their attention on doing good. Here is a business leader who has done well because he set out to do good.

While the main business of companies such as Facebook, Twitter, Craigslist, Groupon and Wikipedia may not be focused on providing aid to those in need or in alleviating poverty, like some of the businesses we look at later, these businesses are inherently social because their core is all about bringing people together, and in many cases it is also their interaction and connectivity that is giving a voice to millions and helping to drive positive change.

We can see the impact social platforms had in the revolutions and protests that swept the Arab world in spring 2011, where the combination of technology, youth and offline protest caused previously unshakeable regimes to topple – and it was a real sign of this new era that a key figure in Egypt was 30-year-old Wael Ghonim, a Google employee leveraging Facebook to help spark the revolution with the 'We are all Khaled Said' page. In recognition of the group's importance in the Arab Spring uprising, Ghonim was named in *Time* magazine's 'Time 100' list of the 100 most influential people of 2011.

The role of social media was critically important in showing people that they were not alone, in organising them, in uniting large groups behind the movement – and also in helping it cascade, like digital dominoes, from one country to the next.

Businesses such as Facebook and Twitter are social businesses in the sense that the social media platforms they have created and made available to all have empowered millions in all kinds of ways, and their collaborative mindset is at the heart of the social revolution.

They are creating social change at an unprecedented rate and this will only continue to accelerate.

Social entrepreneurs from big business

Not all global businesses are headed by forward-thinking leaders like Unilever's Paul Polman or Marks & Spencer's Sir Stuart Rose, who are themselves social entrepreneurs given the entrepreneurial changes they are driving through their companies. But within large corporations there are often senior executives who understand that a move towards social responsibility and sustainability is the way forward. At the Global Social Business Summit in Germany in 2010, delegates were predominately from the non-profit sector, but there were also a number of people from major corporations looking for ways to adopt social business initiatives and apply them to their own businesses.

A senior executive from one of the world's top consumer goods companies said that he was looking for ideas about sustainable ways of creating social benefit. He shared that the global company he works for had shrunk its corporate social responsibility budget during the downturn and that it was now restricted to straightforward philanthropy in the form of charitable donations, disaster relief and the like. He said his biggest issue, as an individual working in a huge organisation, was how to move socially beneficial activities from being part of a siloed CSR operation to being part of the wider business, how to do that in a way that was sustainable, and – most difficult of all – how to convince the wider organisation that it was not only possible but also desirable.

It is one thing when the chief executive of a big company is sold on the premise of socially beneficial business, but there are some companies where those leading the decision-making process are not completely convinced. This makes it incredibly challenging for an executive in that company to get a green light even to experiment.

if you can't change the company, then change company

Clearly, not every business in the world is going to come on board. If executives are frustrated by the lack of willingness within their organisation, then there is another option: if you can't change the company, then change company. Nevertheless, I have personally seen a number of executives who have, over time and through dogged persistence, eventually convinced the rest of the company to come round to their way of thinking. And as the world heads increasingly in this direction, it will become easier to win the battle.

The executive at the summit said he was considering various options but that he didn't really want to operate a distinct 'pilot scheme' set to one side of the business. He wanted to understand how to make what he called the 'jump' from sidelined CSR to incorporating social value into the mainstream business. 'I need to know how to create social benefits in the markets that I am already in and with the products I am already selling,' he said.

While an understandable reaction, a pilot scheme is one way of experimenting to get proof of success: Adidas and Danone are both operating social business schemes, set up as discrete business units. The Danone scheme began after a meeting between Professor Yunus, founder of the Grameen Bank, and Franck Riboud, chairman and chief executive of Groupe Danone, which resulted in the former convincing the latter to invest in a social business. The business provides fortified yogurt to malnourished Bangladeshi children.

One of the benefits of entering the Bangladeshi market and South Asia, where Danone previously had no presence, is that the company can learn more about the market and then apply those learnings to the broader business. So while the social business itself is thought to still be making a loss and has attracted a number of critics, there are other benefits to Groupe Danone. It can also provide valuable learnings, as we have seen from the case of Groupon and its predecessor The Point.

In another example Adidas has also embarked on a joint venture with Grameen, which sells shoes to poor people in Bangladesh for less than one euro a pair. The mission of the Grameen–Adidas company is to make sure that no one, child or adult, goes without shoes.

French water company Veolia has launched a joint social business with Grameen to serve poor people with nutrition and safe drinking water. Germany's BASF SE and Intel of the

USA have entered joint venture social businesses to produce chemically treated mosquito nets and provide information and communication technology for poor people, respectively.

These schemes are not without their critics, and commentators often query the 'purity' of motivation behind some initiatives that involve big business. Some dismiss them as 'tactical' and are sceptical that big business is fundamentally committed. It is easy to criticise a big brand attempting to do good on the grounds that there is something 'in it' for the brand. I would say, firstly, who cares what the motivation is, or whether there might be some benefit to the brand, if the end result is good and creates positive change in the world? Secondly, the whole point is actually that there must be some positive benefit to the business or brand. If we truly want business to change, then socially beneficial business must add value to the company, otherwise it will be impossible to convince the more reluctant companies, shareholders and board members that it is a viable route.

One senior executive working on Adidas's footwear project in Bangladesh described difficulties with NGOs, financial institutions and consumers in developed markets who question how committed big business really is to being part of changing the world. I want to restate my concern about the potential danger that as business genuinely tries to be more responsible, rather than embracing and encouraging that, NGOs and other parties actually distance themselves and criticise the attempts, thereby acting as a major dampener to the movement. Obviously, business needs to be genuine about it. But if it is, then its efforts should be welcomed. I am not suggesting that there should be no scrutiny or accountability, far from it, but if real people who are in need are getting real help in a transparent way, then this has to be a good thing.

My view is that these early drivers of a change of focus within the corporate sector and change for social good should be encouraged at every step.

Yes, there will be failures. No, not everyone's intentions will be as good as they should be. But only the inclusion of the corporate sector in the development of social business will ensure that social business, as a concept, will become truly mainstream and really can help effect positive change in the world.

Social responsibility at the core from the start

Some businesses were created with socially responsible values at their core, and in some cases as their entire *raison d'être*. Outdoor clothing company Patagonia, launched more than 40 years ago, was founded with an ethical and sustainable approach, which at that time was almost unheard of. Its founder Yvon Chouinard insisted on sustainability, proper employee care and products that were designed so that they would not need replacing. The company donates 1% of sales revenue to local environmental groups and in many ways is a model ethical business.

Other businesses, such as Whole Foods and Burt's Bees are good examples in this category of businesses created on a platform of social responsibility. Burt's Bees was founded as a company making home-spun natural products. Now owned by chemical giant Clorox, Burt's Bees was, until recently, led by CEO John Replogle, who joined in 2006 and drove the business to an even greater level of social responsibility, proving it is possible to incorporate socially beneficial activity in a profit-making business.

He led a business that acts transparently, producing natural products in an environmentally sensitive way, and is an active member of the local community of which it is a part. The company has worked with local initiatives to help build homes and a playground for an affordable green housing community in North Carolina, where its headquarters are based. It recently achieved zero waste to landfill status and intends to be a totally zero-waste business by 2020 – a pretty remarkable achievement if they manage it.

Replogle talks about the impact this kind of activity has on employees. He believes that most people want to be good and do good things; all they need is to be given the chance. He says that he doubts whether many of Burt's Bees staff could tell you the revenue figures in the company's results, but every single one of them would be able to talk about the playground Burt's Bees staff built in the local community. The result is that Burt's Bees is a company whose staff feel passionate about working there and have become powerful supporters of the business. They spread the word without being asked to.

Overt consumerism meets social responsibility: looking good and doing good

RED is another interesting example in this space. Set up by Bono and Bobby Shriver, RED pioneered a new business model that created a continuing flow of money from the private sector to raise awareness about HIV and AIDS, by working with corporate partners to produce specific RED products. Apple, for example, created a RED iPod and Nike, Gap, Amex, Converse, Starbucks, Dell and many other brands have been involved, contributing up to 50% of all profits on RED products to the global fund. RED has been criticised by some for a lack of transparency and for too much money being spent on marketing, but it's an interesting and pioneering example of putting overt consumerism alongside doing good. As its mission statement reads: 'RED is a simple idea that transforms our incredible collective power as consumers into a financial force to help others in need.'

The progressive business model was perhaps ahead of its time when RED was launched in 2006, but conscientious consumption is absolutely what people are looking for today. We are now in a decade where if you don't start to do this kind of thing, consumers will increasingly vote against you with the way they spend. I personally think RED's best days are ahead of it: if they manage to retain momentum and keep people interested, they will have a more successful story in this decade than they did in the last one.

Irrespective of RED's critics, the $175 million they have raised since launch cannot be sneered at.

The intersection of social responsibility and social media – the movement generation

The fourth group of social entrepreneurs is perhaps the most interesting and represents the future.

Some are founding enterprises based on principles of transparency and social responsibility; others are creating their own models where profits are shared across all stakeholders. These, often young, social entrepreneurs are driven by a desire to make a difference. It is very common for them to be able to pinpoint a pivotal moment that changed the way they viewed the world or provoked sufficient passion in them to transform a passing thought into concrete, tangible action. In many cases, this has been as a result of global travel, where they saw some of the bigger issues facing people in different parts of the world or simply found the time to get a different perspective on life. Opening themselves up to the world inspired them to create and innovate. My own trip as a 16-year-old around

India opened my eyes to the lives some of the less fortunate people in the world have and was a major factor behind my albeit small efforts to do good.

Adam Braun founded Pencils of Promise, a charity that builds schools in conjunction with the local communities in locations where there is a great need for education. His moment of truth came on a backpacking holiday when he met a child begging on the streets of India. He asked the boy what he wanted most in the world. 'A pencil,' was the reply.

Braun recalls: 'A smile erupted and his eyes brightened. And I saw then the profound power and promise brought through something as small as giving a pencil to just one child. Over the next five years I backpacked through more than 50 countries, handing out thousands of pens and pencils across six continents.'

Many of us, like Duncan Goose who founded One, have been drinking with friends and had a discussion where we put the world to rights. But so few of us translate that kind of conversation into action. The realisation that individual actions can really make a difference to other individuals seems to play an important role in allowing social entrepreneurs to really understand the possibilities. It had such an impact on Goose that he named the brand One to reflect the idea. This organisation works with communities in Africa to address pressing humanitarian needs. It does this by selling a variety of products, including its flagship line One Water. It also licenses the One brand and enters into corporate partnerships. The aim is to make as much profit as possible, which is then invested in social projects.

Goose says: 'There was myself and some other friends who were drunk in a pub in Soho, about five years ago. One of them happened to mention that there were a billion people who didn't have access to clean water. And as a bunch of marketers, why didn't we launch a water brand and give all the profits away, to try and alleviate some of those problems? The reason the brand got called One is that if you're trying to impact on a billion people, it's an impossibility. But actually if you can change one life, one person, one day at a time, then that's a success.' Goose understood this vital concept from his own experience, when in the aftermath of Hurricane Mitch in Honduras he saw the huge impact something as small as a bottle of clean drinking water could have on an individual's life. He says: 'Actually, it doesn't take very much to change somebody's life.'

Other social entrepreneurs have had their own moments of clarity. Ben Ramsden of Pants to Poverty talks of a life-changing trip where he saw the impact of poverty at first hand. Dr Carsten Rübsaamen, who founded Bookbridge, a sustainable business that provides books and education in the developing world, says a visit to rural Mongolia made him reflect on his own good fortune in comparison to what he found there: 'It made me think about the value of education in my own life,' he says. He was inspired to help people without access to education by way of a sustainable social business. Bookbridge helps to set up education centres that are locally owned and operated. Free services are complemented by paid services to local companies and institutions such as language courses and translation services. Bookbridge is an interesting operation as its projects become sustainable within a year.

This is one of the most critical things for social businesses: they must be actual businesses that are able to sustain themselves over the long term. Otherwise, although many projects are clearly worthy endeavours, if they are not sustainable, then they are not businesses in the most fundamental sense and their life expectancy is clearly limited.

Ben Ramsden has a business that is set up to make as much profit as possible, and this profit will be shared across all the stakeholders. Working with thousands of farmers and factory workers in India, Pants to Poverty is creating a way for consumers to buy totally ethically produced cotton clothing. Ben explains: 'The goal of the business is to maximise profits to benefit all of the shareholders in the business.'

Like his peers and much of the Millennial generation, Ramsden has redefined what profit means to them today; it's no longer just financial but also social and environmental, and Ramsden thinks each should be generated equally. And the younger generation is also redefining the notion of 'shareholders', going beyond financial to represent all the stakeholders in the business – farmers, factory workers, retailers, consumers, staff, investors – encompassing the entire value chain community. Ramsden says: 'Therefore, the more profit the business makes, the more positive impact it can create for everyone involved.'

All these businesses have one other key component in common – they are all driven by social media. Some, like Pencils of Promise, use movements of supporters mobilised to raise funds; others, like One, use social media networks to create support and momentum behind their brand to build credibility and consumer demand. Duncan Goose, founder of One, says: 'We believe that social media is fundamentally the way that we are going to enable the world to change by connecting people. We're trying to join up our thinking, join up the world, and join up consumer groups who can, through whatever means they choose, effect change in the world.'

Some challenges for socially responsible startups

Lots of people want to start businesses that are intended to have a social benefit but good intentions are not enough – it is vital for any social initiative to be underpinned by sound business sense and practices. Before he founded Pencils of Promise, Adam Braun spent almost four years learning how to run a successful business and studying how the world of NGOs works.

One of the issues in my view that has faced the not-for-profit sector in the past is that although their intentions were usually exemplary, their execution was not. It is critical for the businesses and operations to be run just as professionally as in the for-profit sector; not only will this help them achieve so much more, but it will also help them avoid one of the biggest criticisms aimed at NGOs – that of waste and not enough of the funds and activities actually reaching those who need them.

Often, at the beginning, an organisation is reliant on volunteers. Adam Braun offers an interesting lesson on how to work with volunteers effectively. He says: 'I think it's a big mistake for a non-profit to assume that someone who is volunteering for you doesn't owe you something as well,' he says. He adds: 'The reality is that they're still occupying your time and your energy and you need to treat them like staff and employees, even if they are volunteers. That is something that it took me probably a year and a half to get to because I was just so thankful that people believed in it early on.'

New socially oriented businesses should be very careful about how the company is registered and set up in the first place. There are myriad schemes and government policies, specific to the country of registration, for social businesses that should be explored early on to avoid problems later.

Have idea, need money

The number-one question for people hoping to create a social business is how to fund it until it becomes sustainable. There are more questions than answers in this context. While lots of aspiring social entrepreneurs have great plans for their business once it is off the ground, few seem able to describe clearly how they are actually going to fund it until such time that it funds itself.

Duncan Goose from One agrees that seeking funding for a not-for-profit business is very difficult, but he sees an alternative: 'Private equity people ask: "What's my return? If I'm going to sink a few million into this, what do I get back?" ... Or you go to a philanthropist or big charity donor and say, "Give us your money and we'll effect change."' Goose believes there is scope for something in between. He says: 'If you could get people to make a side step, that's really where you'll affect the future.'

In September 2010 the Italian business Vita Non Profit Content Company became the first European joint stock company that (by statute) reinvests all its dividends back into the company, to be listed on the stock market. The stock market in question is the Alternative Investment Market (AIM), London, an international market for small to medium-sized companies.

VITA non-profit magazine is dedicated to informing the third sector and was founded in 1994 on the back of an investigation into some of the world's best-known charities. Some might see a paradox in a company that doesn't share its profits with its shareholders competing in a market in which success is measured by shareholder return. But founder and president of the company, Riccardo Bonacina, says there are no inherent legal, economic or even social contradictions to the decision to be listed on the stock market. 'We see our firm identity – made firmer still by our statute – as an asset and we hope to be an example to companies everywhere,' he says.

Many social entrepreneurs think that there should be a completely separate stock market for non-profit businesses. There is no doubt room for a whole range of solutions in this space, and people who are motivated to take part in socially beneficial business activity in any context, within any framework, should be encouraged to do so. Small organisations that begin helping only a few people can have ambitions to multiply and scale their operations. Those in large corporations can introduce sustainable ways that do good and, over time, may see the philosophy behind a pilot scheme extend across the whole of the business.

That said, I think the best way to encourage socially responsible business to become a mainstream movement is to combine positive social change with positive shareholder returns, to prove that not only can you do good and do well but that actually doing good leads to you doing well.

The road ahead

We are at the start of a journey. But there is a new breed of entrepreneur – with its four different types that I outlined earlier – who is accelerating the speed of this journey and leading us down an exciting new path for business. When this new generation of social entrepreneurs are compared with their elders such as Bill Gates, Warren Buffett and Ted Turner, we see some key differences:

First, the younger entrepreneurs base their businesses on openness, free distribution and collaboration. Gates, Buffett and Turner and many of the stand-out businessmen of their generation made their fortunes with a closed protected model.

Second, these twentieth-century entrepreneurs made
their money first and then decided to give back. The new
generation creates their businesses with a view to giving
back from day one.

Now, we should not undermine the significance of what the
older entrepreneurs are doing – and with the creation of the
Giving Pledge they have founded a potentially world-changing
mission, which urges super-wealthy business leaders across
America to pledge at least half their fortunes to charity. Buffett
and Bill and Melinda Gates have put their money where their
mouths are. Buffett has pledged to give away 99% of his
current $45 billion fortune, and the Gates' have pledged to
donate the 'vast majority' of their $54 billion net worth.

But the older generation sees 'giving it away' and doing good
as their end point, whereas the new generation sees that as
their start point. The new generation of social entrepreneurs
understands that in the old world you had to be successful
in business, and then invariably leave your job, in order to
do good as Bill Gates and his super-rich peers have done.
(As an aside, I watched a deft response at Davos two years
ago from the impressive Gates when he was questioned as to
whether the only reason he could do good was that he was
'now free from the clutches of the evil Microsoft'. His reply,
'I am as good or as bad as I have always been', was both
smart and true.) This new generation believes it is because of
their jobs in business that they can do good. And, as I stated
earlier, it isn't just the small business entrepreneurs who
believe this: we are at a turning point where many of the
heads of the biggest businesses believe it too.

I believe this shift in the sense of responsibility that
prevails not only through young entrepreneurs but also
in the Millennial generation in general will provide the
commitment and impetus that the world needs to make
really significant changes for the better.

Today's best social entrepreneurs differ from conventional entrepreneurs in that they want to create social value and financial value – and it is clear that the new entrepreneurs and big business can learn something from each other.

> all elements – the young, the old, big business and new enterprises – need to be able to do good and make money at the same time – because without this, the business of social change will remain a niche activity

The new generation needs to bring the professionalism of the business sector into the social-change and not-for-profit sectors, and big business can learn how to operate in the cause-related field with authenticity, creating movements on social media as they do so. For me, the most important point within all this is that all elements – the young, the old, big business and new enterprises – need to be able to do good and make money at the same time – because without this, the business of social change will remain a niche activity.

The revolutionary shifts in social media and social responsibility are driving massive entrepreneurial change. This is true in the corporate world as well, with individuals in organisations adapting and reinventing themselves for the new landscape. I believe that the biggest area of growth will be where social media intersects with social responsibility, and I think we will see new players here that will come to dominate in the future. They will create a new kind of social responsibility, where everyone in the chain contributes and everyone benefits – as Duncan Niederauer, CEO of the New York Stock Exchange calls it, a 'collaborative social responsibility'.

Ten lessons for and from social entrepreneurs

There are many lessons to be derived from the experience of those already operating in the social business space. Here are some of the key points, as told in their own words.

1 Be bilingual: speak the language of profit and non-profit

One of the most important things for anyone to be successful in this space is they need to be bilingual. They need to speak the language of business and they need to speak the language of non-profit. I just decided to go in to it almost as a wolf in sheep's clothing. I worked at Bain Company consulting in New York for two years to learn as much as I could about how to run a phenomenal organisation one day.

Adam Braun, Pencils of Promise

2 Social media is vital

We believe that social media is fundamentally the way that we are going to enable the world to change by connecting people. We're trying to join up our thinking, join up the world and join up consumer groups who can, through whatever means they choose, effect change in the world.

Duncan Goose, One

3 Be hyper-local: work with local partners

We have to link economic performance and social performance. We learn by doing this with local partners. The way we design plants, the way we design products, the way we design the distribution channels, and the way we work with suppliers. All that was new for us and gives us new ideas.

Olivier Maurel, Groupe Danone

4 Talent is king: employ the right people

As a social venture, Driptech attracts individuals who are already socially minded. Applicants for any given job have for the most part self-selected for social responsibility. In addition, I look for individuals who are creative, honest and hard-working. These are the hardest traits to change in someone, and they are qualities that have worked well as indicators of genuine social responsibility.

Peter Frykman, Driptech inc

5 Volunteers are employees too

One thing I would do differently is I would have put in a hard measure of accountability on volunteers from the start. I think it's a big mistake for a non-profit to assume that someone who is volunteering for you doesn't owe you something as well. The reality is that they're still occupying your time and your energy and you need to treat them like staff and employees, even if they are volunteers.

Adam Braun, Pencils of Promise

6 Collaborate with consumers

Collaboration is a better way to interact with the consumers. They want to help create what they consume and say: 'I did this, this was my idea.' We, as companies, will be more and more facilitators of that than producers or sellers.

Gianpaolo Grazioli, Giapo

7 Be open: partnership is more important than ownership

Partnership has challenges: realising people's motivations and making sure that they are met; not being in control as much as you want to be. Our advertising, legal, finance, even our fundraising, the whole production of the product, PR – all partnership. Everything. So it's about managing those relationships. It takes away a level of control that you would normally have. But the benefit is that immense creativity often comes out of it. And it's about realising that we can't do it all alone. And why on earth should we? Why do we need to own this? We just need to facilitate it.

Ben Ramsden, Pants to Poverty

8 Leverage the power of youth

I think innovation is at the core of a lot of this movement. Innovation really stems from the belief that something which everyone else assumes is impossible can be made possible. And there is no one else who is naive enough to make that assumption and then go prove it, in the way that youth does. That is something that a lot of big business overlooks – the power of the youth to catalyse movements.

Adam Braun, Pencils of Promise

9 Don't be afraid to make money

To create the greatest social impact we must be financially successful so that we can scale sustainably. Being profitable not only ensures sustainability but helps attract more commercial players to design products as well. As socially responsible organisations achieve financial success, there will be competition from businesses duplicating our approach, and the world will benefit.

Peter Frykman, Driptech inc

10 Think big

This is the future of business. This is new business and we will do to all business what new media did to media.

Ben Ramsden, Pants to Poverty

We-volution: how collaboration is changing business

If you want to go fast, go alone; if you want to go far, go together.

African proverb

Who shares wins

One of the key things that the social entrepreneurs we looked at in the previous chapter have in common – from Mark Zuckerberg at Facebook to Andrew Mason at Groupon to Jimmy Wales at Wikipedia – is a belief in openness, transparency and collaboration. They understood and leveraged its phenomenal power in the businesses that they created.

There are those who look at the world of radical transparency that social media has created – and with it the ability of large groups of consumers to collaborate and drive business in the direction in which they want it to go – as an extremely concerning threat. At the same time, however, it presents a unique and unprecedented opportunity to work with people to create the products, experiences and services of the future and is one of the most exciting new frontiers in business today.

The leaders and companies that understand this and leverage the enormous potential of collaboration that the digital era enables will have very bright futures. A business may not have been created from day one to be a Facebook, Groupon or Wikipedia, but it can benefit by learning from them.

More and more, consumers are having a say in what business does, making themselves heard by telling companies what it is they want and expect from them. They want business to be responsive. They want companies to be more sustainable and more socially responsible. Together, they will drive businesses to become the sort of companies that they want them to be.

And, they no longer want to just accept what they are given: they want to play a part in creating, shaping and tailoring the products they buy. The architecture of the digital world invites collaboration; after all, the very origins of the internet come from the desire to share information. And I believe that the Social Brand is the model of the future, one that connects people more intimately with brands, entices collaboration and fuels creative participation.

Collaborative production: from new product development to social product development

Prosumers, the proactive, empowered and engaged consumers discussed in Chapter 2, are at the forefront of this movement. One of the most successful stories of people designing products for themselves is the mountain bike, which was 'invented' by a group of bike enthusiasts in Marin County, northern California.

It's an interesting story about people creating something with little idea that the outcome would be a worldwide phenomenon. They scavenged pre-Second World War bikes from junkshops, customised and tailored them, and then rode them down the slopes of the local mountain. Challenges between local groups eventually sparked media coverage and what started out as a mud-splattered hobby became a multibillion-dollar industry, an industry that began by consumers designing and adapting a product in the way they wanted.

At the height of its popularity in the mid-1980s, the mountain bike accounted for 60% of all bicycle store sales (in the USA). Even today, now that the market has matured, the figure sits at about 28% of the $6 billion US market (according to estimates from the National Bicycle Dealers Association) – which is probably a little bit larger than those early pioneers throwing themselves down mountains on reconditioned bikes would have imagined at the time.

> the next decade will see a much greater level of collaboration between consumers and brands

The next decade will see a much greater level of collaboration between consumers and brands. The mountain bike may have come about accidentally with people inventing something that was then adopted by manufacturers, but more and more consumers now expect to be involved in the process and want to play a key role in shaping the products they will buy. The new world puts consumers ahead of the producers and facilitates social product development, where technology allows consumers to input and shape, co-create and co-market the products they buy.

From B2C to C2B

With this we will see a shift from an old business-to-consumer (B2C) world – with the all-powerful company deciding which products to create and manufacture – to the new consumer-to-business (C2B) world, where the all-powerful consumer will shape the products they consume.

An interesting early example of this is from PepsiCo in the UK, with their 'Do Us a Flavour' collaboration for Walkers crisps (known as Lay's in other markets). Back in 2008, the Walkers brand was flagging in the UK in the face of increasing competition. In response, Walkers decided to involve consumers in the product development with a major campaign asking people to send in their ideas for new flavours. The top six flavours were then launched and the nation was asked to decide which they preferred. There were real rewards on offer too: a £50,000 prize and 1% of all future profits for the winning flavour. In total 1.2 million entries were submitted, at an incredible rate of 156 per second at its peak. Once the six shortlisted flavours were launched, each was promoted like an individual candidate in an election campaign, with its own TV ad and social media platform, where it 'campaigned' for votes. Online forums hosted heated debates about which flavour was best. Yahoo TV filmed an ongoing election news series and 810,000 votes were cast.

Overall, it was a great success, with year-on-year sales rising by 14%. The company has since run a similar collaboration for Lay's in India: 'Give Us Your Dillicious Flavour', with a response number of 1.3 million that outperformed the UK – although clearly India's population is somewhat larger.

PepsiCo's initiative is a great example of how things have changed. And this change will not only extend across what kinds of product people want, but also impact the fundamental relationship that consumers have with brands – as in the words of Oliver Twist, they will want 'more': more involvement in the design of products, more customisation and tailoring to their requirements, more of a voice in the communication campaigns of the brands they love, more responsive and connected companies delivering a more personalised customer service, and much more information about the values of the company or brand they are buying from.

A dis-industrial revolution?

Interestingly, with this change comes a new set of issues. The world built by the Industrial Revolution gave us mass production and success came from an economies-of-scale manufacturing model, delivering cheaper and cheaper products in larger and larger homogenised quantities. The social revolution is going to give us collaborative production.

This is, in general, not an issue for service industries, but for manufacturing businesses it throws up many questions. The consumer is beginning to have an expectation that the best businesses will respond to their individual needs. If we say that collaborative means more tailored and personalised manufacturing, then the economies of scale driven by mass production come under threat.

Will the social revolution challenge the very basis of success for the Industrial Revolution as the manufacturing industry faces a dis-industrial revolution and businesses start going back to smaller, individual production runs, losing the enormous benefits of mass standardised production?

> the social revolution will empower the consumer in the way that the Industrial Revolution empowered the corporation

I think it's pretty clear that the answer is no – modern business is too smart and efficient for that. Instead, the big difference will be that the social revolution will empower the consumer in the way that the Industrial Revolution empowered the corporation. And the most successful companies will be those that best collaborate with the digitally empowered consumer.

A glimpse of the future of collaborative production may come from looking at some of the innovative but still embryonic business models.

Made.com is an online furniture retailer with a community where members design, vote for and then actually produce items in collaboration. Users and young designers are encouraged to submit their designs. The best designs are developed into prototypes and then posted on to the website, where they are voted on by the Made community. The most popular pieces are then available for pre-order, made in China, shipped by container and delivered directly to buyers – combining the benefit of totally original designs with prices way below those on the high street.

In another example, one of my fellow Young Global Leaders from the World Economic Forum, Kohei Nishiyama, founded CUUSOO.com. CUUSOO.com brings together inventors, manufacturers and consumers. Inventors submit their designs. Manufacturers state the price at which they can make the product based on a certain volume. And then when enough people have said they want the product, it gets made. It isn't only inventors but also ordinary people who can submit ideas and get help from the community of 20,000 members with refinements and improvements to those ideas. A number of products have been successfully produced, notably in conjunction with retailer Muji and toy brand Lego. None of them to date, however, has achieved mass-market numbers. Is this because we are at the very early stages of a new behaviour? Or because the idea, although great in theory, doesn't work in practice? The legendary Steve Jobs used to argue the latter. He was famous for not asking consumers what they wanted, but instead just delivering what he believed was right – or, put another way, delivering what they didn't yet know they would want. When asked what consumer and market research Apple did to guide the development of new products, Jobs stated: 'None. It isn't the consumers' job to know what they want.'

Time will tell. What is clear is that the consumer has been empowered to give their input and feedback in ways that were unimaginable only a decade ago and in doing so created both a major challenge and an opportunity to meet their expectations.

Collaboration to enhance a product experience

If you don't want to go as far as allowing consumers to actually co-design products, another way of leveraging collaboration is to use it to add value, in the biggest sense, to the overall product experience and to the brand's relationship with its consumers.

One great example of this is Sneakerpedia, from shoe retailer Foot Locker. They are basically trying to create the biggest archive of sneakers – or trainers – ever assembled, by asking sneaker fans and obsessives to share about their shoes on a global hub called Sneakerpedia. Users take a picture of the sneaker, tag it, and add the shoe's history and a description right down to minute details such as stitching types and materials. The database also incorporates multiple search options, for example allowing users to look for which shoe a particular celebrity likes.

What is interesting about Sneakerpedia is that it is not designed to sell anything. Foot Locker says it is 'a community place, not a market place' that is run 'by sneakerheads, for sneakerheads'.

Another example of using the power of the crowd to enhance the customer's experience is from Uniqlo, with their Uniqlooks app for the iPhone. Uniqlo describes this as 'a social communication platform where people can share their own Uniqlo style'. The idea is for people to mix and match Uniqlo pieces to create bold and interesting looks that they then share. Fellow members from all around the world can check out each other's looks and comment, and the most popular looks are rewarded by top fashion and design specialists.

Although neither of these initiatives will generate any immediate sales for Sneakerpedia and Uniqlo, they are a great way of showing their passion for, in the one case, sneakers and, in the other, fashion, and they will generate increased loyalty from their customers and with that future sales. They are examples of giving consumers something for nothing, in the belief that down the line it will pay back.

But digital technology's ability to enable collaboration hasn't just changed how products are designed, produced and marketed – it's changed how they are consumed as well.

CASE STUDY

Nike+: collaborating on three levels

A great example that combines a lot of these principles is Nike+. This is a three-tier collaboration – Nike with Apple, Nike with the runner, and the runner with other runners.

Nike with Apple

The first collaboration is between two companies. Nike collaborated with Apple to create a chip built into a running shoe that allows runners to track the distance, pace and calories burned on a run.

The shoe device 'talks' to the runner's iPod, which then sends the athlete's running data to the web. Each time the athlete runs, information – distance, pace, time and calories burned – can be loaded onto the Nike+ runners' website.

Nike with the runner

Once the runner has sent their information to the Nike+ website, all the data are stored and a tool creates charts and graphics so that progress can be monitored over time and goals set. And there are Nike+ Coach training schedules created by professional coaches to help them train for an event or particular distance.

There is also a GPS-enabled iPhone app that can be used to enhance individual workouts with users 'cheered' as they run.

They can also create a Nike+ Mini, an animated alter ego that takes on a life of its own as training progresses.

And they can get involved in organised challenges, create their own challenges and connect with other runners in the Nike+ community, which leads to the third collaboration.

Runner with runner: the world's largest running club

The website has enabled Nike+ to facilitate a community of runners – all centred around the Nike brand – which allows them to connect with each other, challenging each other and comparing performances. Nike+ Map allows runners to load maps of where they run, share them with others and try routes that others recommend.

The app enables them to broadcast to their friends while running and to take part in the wider social aspects of Nike+.

The Nike+ community has built its own dynamic, full of challenges, competition, validation and friendship. In August 2008, for example, 800,000 runners logged on and signed up to run a 10 km race sponsored by Nike, which occurred simultaneously in 25 cities worldwide.

Nike+ gives consumers a way to engage with the brand, with each other, and to tell Nike what it is they want. It allows the company to create and sell products with a lower risk of failure, as the community has asked for them. When runners started asking Nike for T-shirts to commemorate milestones of mileages run, Nike was happy to oblige.

Initially limited only to Nike shoes, Nike subsequently opened up the use of the shoe device so it can fit in any shoe, not just the Nike brand. This is a smart move that demonstrates Nike understands the power of sharing and being open in today's world – it's also in keeping with the company's move from being all about a 'better shoe' to being about a 'better you' and one where it has defined 'athlete' as 'anyone who has a body'.

Nike's view is that even if someone doesn't buy its shoes, the passion they see that Nike has for running will eventually lead them to buy something from Nike – and this philosophy is supported by the data – Nike has said that the average customer value of people on Nike+ is significantly higher than the norm.

We-commerce

Groupon is a very interesting example of this, where mass collective purchasing power is brought to bear to force prices down. Proof of the incredible potential for collaborative consumption comes from the fact that Groupon is cited as being the fastest company in the history of America to reach $1 billion in revenue.

The group-buying model that offers a deal of the day in hundreds of local areas is based entirely on connections – Groupon's connections with local retailers, and the buyers' collective power – and it leverages the power of sociability and location. Groupon's founder, social entrepreneur Andrew Mason, has already turned down cash offers from Yahoo! and more recently Google was reportedly offering $6 billion.

Groupon has achieved impressive scale very quickly, and in my view has the most enormous potential, combining as it does, the sexy image of a digital business with the cold hard cash of the bricks-and-mortar world.

To infinity and beyond

Groupon also shows an interesting way forward for Facebook, especially given that Facebook already knows what you like – because you've told them – so they know what deals to offer you. Despite the massive success of Facebook and undoubted power in generating a huge global user base of over 600 million people and counting, relatively speaking, Facebook's revenue base has lagged far behind. If Facebook leverages the potential collective bargaining power of its vast audience and overlays location-based offers, then world domination is nigh. Or perhaps, more accurately, world domination from a revenue perspective as well as its current image perspective. This opportunity will be even greater when the mobile phone replaces the wallet as the payment vehicle of choice.

To date, the majority of our business models haven't been based on a genuine understanding of the power of massive collaboration. The great strength of digital technology is its ability to accumulate millions and millions of individual actions that, while small in their own right, have an enormous impact when combined (see the case study on p. 116). This 'mass individualism' is in my view where enormous potential lies.

We Feel Fine

A great example of using technology to create a giant global digital collaboration is We Feel Fine (www.wefeelfine.org). This is a brilliant idea today, but when you consider it was created in 2005, it is groundbreaking. An algorithm was created that reaches out into the internet and social media world to search for and collate all posts and comments beginning with 'I feel' or 'I am feeling' to create a real-time global database of human feeling. The interface, called a self-organising particle system, represents each feeling with a floating coloured dot.

Any particle or dot can be clicked on to reveal the full sentence or photograph it relates to. The particles zoom around wildly until asked to self-organise along a number of axes, which then correlate various emotions. The feelings can be viewed in a number of different ways: from a scrolling list of feelings, to viewing all of the photos posted with the feelings, to groupings by types of feeling, to showing metrics for the most representative feelings in the past few hours.

The founders, Jonathan Harris and Sep Kamvar, released the book *We Feel Fine: An Almanac of Human Emotion* at the end of 2009. Both this and the website are based on the premise that people are very honest in their blogs and it can realistically be described as a reflection of humanity online.

It is described as an 'artwork that is authored by everyone' and it is both beautiful and fascinating. Its implications are much wider than simply the creation of hypnotic art – if you can mine what people are feeling at a particular time and correlate reasons why, then there are huge opportunities for commercial use of this type of data.

The data collection engine at the heart of We Feel Fine is one of its most interesting aspects. It holds a database of several million human feelings, increasing by 15,000–20,000 new feelings per day. Because posts and blogs are structured in largely standard ways, the age, gender and geographical location of the author can usually be extracted from the profile information and saved along with the sentence, as can the local weather conditions at the time the sentence was written. All of this information is saved.

Technology allows something to be done at a breadth and scale that would be impossible for even thousands of humans to achieve – and it does it in real time. The feelings can be searched and sorted across a number of demographic slices, offering responses to specific questions such as 'Do Europeans feel sad more often than Americans?' 'Do women feel fat more often than men?' 'Does rainy weather affect how we feel?' 'What are the most representative feelings of female New Yorkers in their twenties?' 'What do people feel right now in Baghdad?' 'What were people feeling on Valentine's Day?' 'Which are the happiest cities in the world?' 'The saddest?' The potential is limitless and we will see numerous businesses over the next decade start to use what people are saying in social media to create and deliver better products and services and more relevant messages.

To give a concrete example, imagine Facebook were to strike a deal with Starbucks so that every time someone checks in on Facebook at their local Starbucks and buys a coffee, Starbucks pays Facebook 0.1% of the purchase price. Bear in mind that near-field communication (NFC) technology that is now arriving on the market and allowing people to pay with their mobile phones will make this very easy to operationalise. Although on the surface this is a very small amount of money, if you multiply that by the number of cups of coffee being sold each day by that Starbucks outlet, and then by the number of days in the year, and then imagine doing the same thing in every Starbucks in the USA and then maybe adding in the rest of the world – a rough calculation based on the 2.3 billion cups sold per year would yield over $10 million. And then imagine heading off and doing a similar deal with every other major food outlet in the world. It isn't hard to see how something that starts by looking like a ridiculously small sum very quickly adds up to a massive revenue stream, especially as technology's ability to cope with it would allow you to do this not only with massive global companies but also with small local retailers. And now imagine combining that with group buying offers and friend recommendations and location-based targeting, and it's easy to see just how enormous a revolution is awaiting the world of retail. And I'm sure someone smarter than me will work out much better models than this.

In simple terms, if the Industrial Revolution's success was based on mass production and unlocking the potential of producing millions of things in exactly the same way, then the social revolution's success may well be based upon a new kind of mass consumption, consuming millions of things but often in an infinite number of different ways and places.

Cutting out the corporation

Another big difference of the social revolution is that it doesn't only revolutionise relationships between companies and people; it also revolutionises relationships between people themselves.

In fact, eBay, one of the earliest examples of success in the internet space, was based around this kind of collaborative consumption among people. Interestingly, eBay was founded in 1995, the same year as another big collaborative success, Craigslist. Both of these models differ from the examples above in that they aren't collective ways of buying manufacturers' products, but instead they are actually peer-to-peer models that cut out the company.

Rachel Botsman in her book *What's Mine Is Yours: How Collaborative Consumption Is Changing the Way We Live* predicts that direct negotiation between ordinary people on a localised basis will grow significantly over the coming years.

And I happen to agree with her. The combination of the effects of the financial crisis, concern over our impact on the environment and the desire to consume better has greatly driven the focus on conscientious consumption. And this move is being driven at an increasing pace by prosumers and the Millennials. Clearly one of the most conscientious ways of consuming is not to consume at all – or at the very least either to borrow or share a product or to pass on goods we no longer need. Today's technology now allows us to easily find, trust and match with other people offering goods and services – so the need to 'own' that drove the excesses and consumption-driven society of the 1980s will give way to an openness to share that will be one of the fastest-growing movements of this decade. If 'own' was the word of the 1980s, then 'share' will be the word for this decade. And interestingly, a society that evolved from 'needs' to 'wants' over the previous centuries will start asking itself again whether it really 'needs' to buy something after all.

There's no 'I' in 'we'

JCDecaux's Vélib' bike-sharing programme in Paris is built on these principles and has been a major success, allowing people to rent a bike in central Paris for upwards of 30 minutes – with numerous stations around the city making it very easy to take out and return the bikes.

My boss, Groupe Bolloré and Havas chairman, Vincent Bolloré, is moving this to the next level by funding an electric car project in Paris to launch late in 2011. The business, called Autolib, will provide 3000 electric vehicles and install 1000 charging stations across the city centre and suburbs of Paris. It will run in a very similar way to the city bike scheme. For a usage fee, drivers will be able to use the cars and return them to any charging station. It's a great way to cut down on congestion, reduce parking problems and allow all residents of Paris to have access to a car without having to buy one, while at the same time converting to electric vehicles and reducing pollution – with reports saying the system could reduce carbon dioxide emissions by 22,000 tons a year.

There are already a number of other interesting examples of collaborative consumption around the world – from Airbnb, a social bed and breakfast site that allows you to rent a room in 13,216 cities across 181 countries from a 'real person' like you, to Zopa, which allows social lending, matching people looking to borrow money with people prepared to lend it and, as their website says, 'Cutting out the banks, everybody gets a better deal', to Swap.com, a twenty-first-century digital version of a famous kids' TV programme when I was growing up called *Multi-Coloured Swap Shop*, which allows people to list what they have but no longer want and swap it for something they do want across a vast number of categories.

There are also many business models that seem too niche to be successful, such as Supermarmite.com, which enables you to use location-based applications to share what you are cooking and see whether people living near you are prepared to pay to eat some of it. But note to Supermarmite.com: please feel free to gloat and say I told you so when your IPO is a dramatic success and you are worth more than Google.

What all these businesses have in common is that they leverage social and digital technology to connect people in new ways and create new markets.

The power of we – collaborative consumption models

▌ **Zopa** – a social lending marketplace matching people looking to borrow money with those prepared to lend. Loans are low-cost, and no middle man means better rates for all. Terms are tough though, and only those with great credit ratings need apply.

▌ **Tourboarding** – experience China for free by swapping a couple of hours of English language training. In return get free room and board or a string of other services, such as tour guiding and Chinese language instruction.

▌ **Zipcar** – the world's largest car club. Members, or Zipsters, can reserve cars by the hour or the day. Using a Zipcard they can unlock the car and drive. Discounts and deals with local retailers and restaurants are also part of the package.

▌ **TaskRabbit** – users post a task that needs doing, such as gardening, painting or deliveries. 'Runners' and local tradespeople bid for the job. Users select the best bid. Job done. This currently runs in five major US cities.

▌ **CouchSurfing** – an international network that connects travellers with local people and communities around the world. Started in 2003 as a simple link between travellers and people willing to have guests in their homes, it now incorporates an array of activities, social networking and events.

▌ **SubMate** – a service that aims to give commuters on the Paris, Barcelona, Hong Kong, London, Madrid, New York and Bilbao underground routes new things to do. Register a regular route and it connects fellow travellers who can then meet up for things to do and deals to take advantage of.

▌ **Hyperlocavore** – users can share gardens, tools, seeds, know-how and labour to grow food. Social gardening!

▌ **Chegg** – students can share and rent textbooks and study materials for courses.

▌ **thredUP** – a major parents' and toddlers' group where you can swap boxes of children's clothing and toys. Lenders are rated to help parents pick the right boxes.

▌ **SplitStuff** – a site to help organise local projects and groups of individuals to make joint purchases. Users can buy goods, equipment and services in bulk and split costs.

Collective good

And while people might not get that excited about collaborating around what they are having for dinner on a particular night, they do around the causes and issues that they care about. And it's here that social media's huge power to organise mass movements of people across the globe and unite them behind a common goal really comes to bear.

Perhaps the greatest example of this is my friend and One Young World Counsellor, Oscar Morales. Oscar is the creator of One Million Voices Against FARC and headed the largest anti-terrorism demonstration in the history of the world. Oscar, then a 33-year-old engineer, was sick of the killing, kidnapping and murder being carried out by FARC, a revolutionary guerrilla organisation based in Colombia.

So one day, from his home in Barranquilla on Colombia's Caribbean coast, he started a Facebook group against FARC. The rest, as they say, is history. The speed of takeup was phenomenal. As Oscar says: 'When I created the group, I remember that I invited my network of friends – no more than 500 people. But to my surprise, after 12 hours, there were 1500 members that had joined the group. The next day there were 4000 members. The next day, 9000 members. At the end of the week it was 150,000 members and now we come with almost half a million users.'

The movement was taken up by newspapers and radio and television stations across the country and beyond. The marches against FARC were organised through Facebook in less than a month and, with the support of thousands of volunteers, flooded the streets with 12 million people in over 200 cities and 40 different countries on 4 February 2008.

Oscar says: 'When we proposed the march, in a matter of minutes people were already joining, and in just one month we had already convinced 12 million people to go out on the streets and the internet was the best tool for doing that.' Oscar also talked about the important role of traditional media in ensuring global reach.

No one was more amazed than Oscar at the results of his actions, and he encourages others to do the same: 'Believe in yourself. Believe me, you have the power, it is within yourself, you just have to start,' he says. 'It doesn't matter if only one person follows you on the first day; the next day there will be five more. If you believe in something, do it; don't expect someone else to do it for you. Take the first step and you will be amazed at the power of your energy and thoughts.'

Oscar has been described by Facebook as the 'ultimate Facebooker' and by Hillary Clinton as creating the 'single biggest anti-terrorism demonstration in history'. I first met Oscar when we both spoke at Google Zeitgeist in the UK in 2009. He was there with Jared Cohen, then the 27-year-old head of counter-terrorism and espionage in Hillary Clinton's State Department. Cohen told the story of how the US administration had been stunned by this movement against FARC and had tried to track down who was behind it. In the end, after much searching, Cohen had simply gone on Facebook and friended Oscar. As Cohen explained: 'I sent Oscar a Facebook message, and I said are you the one that did this and did you know that the *Wall Street Journal* wrote about you today? And I told Oscar that I wanted to come down to Colombia and meet with him. It was, I think, the very first diplomatic engagement in the history of the US government via an online social network.'

Cohen's experience of social media and digital technology in government is both interesting and demonstrative of the speed of change: 'When I arrived in the Department of State in September 2006, I would argue that we as a government were infected with what I would describe as digital media giggle syndrome. Meaning, you couldn't go to a serious meeting and talk about Facebook or Google or any of these digital platforms without fear of being laughed out of the room. Now I would argue that ... especially under Secretary Clinton, if you're not bringing up technology in every single meeting, whether it's about public diplomacy, or development or political or economic issues, then you're not doing what the Secretary of State wants us to do.'

Oscar's actions were an interesting precursor to the Arab Spring of 2011, where young people empowered by

technology created a wave of revolution across the Middle
East. They are also a demonstration of the key role that
social media plays in driving traditional media. People today
want to act; the digital revolution not only has given them
a powerful tool to do so but also allows them to see quickly
that they are not alone, as hundreds, thousands or, in Oscar's
case, millions sign up to the cause.

In line with this we are seeing more and more social cause
initiatives appearing around the world. As mentioned in
Chapter 4, Facebook founder Chris Hughes launched Jumo,
and its recent merger with GOOD may help them gain
even more momentum. And Hollywood actor Ed Norton
created Crowdrise, a platform for non-profit fundraising and
volunteering, which he was inspired to do after he raised
$1.2 million in less than eight weeks by organising and
running in the Maasai Marathon. Not surprisingly, Facebook
has launched Facebook Causes.

One of the key points for businesses to take from this is that
the same power of collaborative movements to unite behind
causes can and will also be used against your brand or
business if you don't act in the way today's prosumers and
Millennials want you to.

It's perhaps a slight irony that Facebook's ability to create
powerful social movements has been recently turned back
on it. Greenpeace launched a Facebook page to put pressure
on Facebook to use 100% renewable energy. Over 300,000
people joined the movement and it achieved a Guinness
World Record for the most comments in 24 hours on a
Facebook page. The overall campaign, which included data
reports on energy use, has had a significant effect, with
Facebook saying it takes the data seriously and will share
more information and consider the carbon impact in any
future locations. It has also invited Greenpeace members
to take part in its Open Compute Project, which is itself a

collaboration aimed at helping to reduce environmental impact.

Open source drives collaboration

My own first major experience of driving collaboration around a cause was for Kofi Annan with the tck tck tck Time for Climate Justice campaign targeting the climate talks at Copenhagen.

I was introduced to Annan by Hervé de Clerck from ACT Responsible – a non-profit organisation whose aim is to show the positive role of advertising in social and environmental issues – who told me that the former Secretary-General of the UN was looking for an agency for his campaign to highlight the issue of injustice around climate change.

After an inspirational meeting with Annan in Geneva, we signed up to help. The goal was to put pressure on the world's leaders to deliver a binding climate agreement at the UN summit in Copenhagen.

The observation I made when looking at what everyone had been doing about climate change was that although there were some terrific campaigns, they all seemed to be working in isolation or, even worse, sometimes in competition with one another.

My recommendation was that instead of competing, we should all work together and collaborate. And my idea was simple: to create an open-source campaign. In fact, we set out to create the largest open-source campaign in the world.

The 'tck tck tck' logo was the foundation of the campaign and it was designed to represent the ticking of a clock – written of course in twenty-first-century SMS-speak. It was a powerful way to communicate the counting down of the deadline to the Copenhagen climate talks and also the counting down to the deadline on the world's future if we didn't act on the critical issue of climate. Additionally, on a subliminal level it just happens to be the noise a bomb makes – and if we don't act, then the whole issue of climate change is a bomb waiting to go off. Our goal was also to create a movement rather than a campaign and the ticking of a clock represented that very nicely.

We presented to the Global Campaign for Climate Action and got them on board with the idea of using 'tck' across all of their different campaigns. The next step was to ask the world's marketing and advertising industry to join us. Kofi Annan came with Bob Geldof to the Cannes Lions Advertising Festival, and we made an appeal to the world's advertisers and marketers to use the 'tck' logo on everything they were doing between September and the climate talks in December. The appeal was simple – if you're an advertiser we ask you to run the logo on your advertising, your website, in store; if you're an agency, we want you to create content and push it out there; if you're an individual, we want you to sign the 'tck' petition, download the track, put the twibbon on your twitter feed, put the logo on Facebook; and if you're a media owner, we want you to give us free media.

As part of the campaign we recorded a new version of Midnight Oil's 'Beds Are Burning' with stars and celebrities, including Duran Duran, Mark Ronson, Jamie Cullum, Mélanie Laurent, Marion Cotillard, Milla Jovovich, Fergie, Lily Allen, Manu Katché, Bob Geldof, Youssou N'Dour, Yannick Noah and many others. Peter Garrett of Midnight Oil, who wrote the original lyrics, rewrote them for us so they were relevant to climate change (the original song had been about Aboriginal land rights) and gave us permission to use the track for free. But the track wasn't only the campaign anthem: every time someone downloaded the song, it also represented a signature on a giant digital petition.

Overall more than 18 million people signed up as climate allies, and governments endorsed the campaign worldwide, with then Prime Minister Gordon Brown and the UK government officially calling on UK business leaders and celebrities to support the campaign. Over $30 million of media coverage ran across 60 countries. If you type 'tck tck tck' into the Google search bar today there are literally thousands and thousands of images of 'tck' use around the world – probably only 1% of which were created by us.

'tck' became one of the largest social movements in history.

Despite that, the world's leaders failed to deliver, underlining the disconnection that too often exists between politicians and the world's people. The world's people wanted action. The world's leaders failed to act, instead becoming embroiled in political standoffs and posturing.

What 'tck' does show, however, is the benefit of collaborating and acting together, rather than acting alone. And the power of open-source movements.

The smartest brains are often outside of your organisation

> one of the key questions everyone should be asking themselves today is, 'Who could I collaborate and work with to get better results?'

This should be a guiding principle for every modern business. One of the key questions everyone should be asking themselves today is, 'Who could I collaborate and work with to get better results?' A lot of the time the smartest brains are actually outside of the company.

In his book *Wikinomics*, Don Tapscott – another One Young World Counsellor – tells a great story about a gold mine operated by Goldcorp in Red Lake, Ontario, which was beset with problems and facing collapse. The likelihood was that the mine would be forced to close, which would mean the end of Goldcorp. Despite there being evidence of rich gold deposits, the company's geologists had failed to provide an accurate estimate of the gold's value or its exact location. The then chief executive Rob McEwen heard the story of Linus Torvalds, the Finnish inventor of the open-source computer operating system Linux, which was created after Torvalds opened up his code, allowing thousands of developers to work on it and make contributions of their own.

McEwen decided to go against one of the fundamental principles of mining, which is that geological data are top secret and carefully guarded. His idea was to open up all Goldcorp's data to the world by publishing the data online, thinking that if his own geologists could not find the gold then maybe someone else could.

The 'Goldcorp Challenge', launched in 2000, offered $575,000 in prize money to anyone who could successfully pinpoint where the undiscovered gold might be located. Hundreds of people took part, including retired geologists and students. Between them they recommended 110 locations, four-fifths of which turned out to be correct. The company's value soared from $100 million to $9 billion.

If it is unexpected that a business would be so open, then it's even less expected that someone from the CIA would be. However, that was the case for former CIA Deputy Director of Intelligence, Carmen Medina. A prolific blogger and tweeter, Medina, now retired, has ideas that seem to go against everything the CIA is meant to embody, such as covert operations and secrecy.

She is however in favour of an open network that makes the same intelligence available to thousands of CIA analysts. The idea is that the more people that look at something, the more likely it is that someone will make an unexpected and valuable contribution. She says of CIA analysts: 'Their business is to make sense of the world and it's really hard to do that in a closed network.'

Some of Medina's ideas resulted in the 2005 launch of Intellipedia, an online wiki system for sharing data used by the US intelligence networks. It consists of three versions, each with different levels of classification – top secret, secret, and sensitive but unclassified.

The system goes some way to addressing concerns that followed the post-mortem of events that led up to the Iraq invasion, based on flawed intelligence. Had there been strong dissenting opinions and other perspectives voiced, then a different path might have been followed – imagine the impact if the timing of Wikileaks had been different. Intellipedia is now used widely by a young intelligence workforce that is familiar with an online world and how it operates.

Medina had understandable issues in trying to convince the intelligence community that sharing information was a good idea. In fact, she says, many colleagues regarded her and her team as 'heretics'. Those in business have no such excuse; in many cases the commercial case for opening up access to information is compelling. And in the same way as Julian Assange came along with Wikileaks and decided he would share the information anyway, someone will do the same thing to your business if you don't.

A problem shared is a problem solved

The idea of bringing together as many minds as possible
is spreading in some of the most unexpected places and
in surprising ways. The US Navy, through the Office
of Naval Research, has developed a multiplayer game
called MMOWGLI, which stands for Massive Multiplayer
Online WarGame Leveraging the Internet, through which
it hopes to develop strategies to combat, in its first
iteration, modern-day pirates off the coast of Somalia.
The plan is to bring together a disparate group of players
– experts drawn from academia, defence, government
and non-government organisations – in the hope that the
intellectual range will identify new solutions to seemingly
intractable problems.

It's not the first time that the public has been asked to help
in unearthing wrongdoing. During the UK MPs' expenses
scandal, where politicians were caught claiming expenses
they shouldn't have been claiming, the *Guardian* newspaper
created a system that allowed the public to search through
700,000 documents to look at who had been claiming what.
More than 20,000 people took part.

Greenpeace is also calling on the public to help it analyse
documents. It made hundreds of Freedom of Information
requests to the US government related to the BP oil-spill
disaster. It obtained more than 30,000 pages of documents
but didn't have the resources to go through them all, and so
it has appealed for help. The documents have been loaded
on to a website and categorised so that people interested in
different aspects of the case can easily access the documents,
review them and share the key findings.

The new collaborative world

Once you open your mind to collaborative approaches it changes your whole outlook. Your solutions become different and in my experience invariably better.

It's a world where fierce rivals like the *Guardian*, the *New York Times*, *Der Spiegel*, *Le Monde* and *El País* work together on projects like the Wikileaks cables and are now looking for ways in which to harness their collective resources again.

It's a world where national leaders Barack Obama, David Cameron and Nicolas Sarkozy get together and write an article about the situation in Libya for the *New York Times* that carries a joint byline. And where UK Prime Minister Cameron holds a webcast with Mark Zuckerberg to use Facebook to reach out to the UK's citizens and ask for their ideas on reducing the national debt.

It's a world where people get together and collaborate, creating new markets and cutting out the middleman.

It is a world where companies like Unilever and Nestlé are working in cooperation with NGOs such as Greenpeace in an effort to source sustainable palm oil. Not so long ago, that sort of collaboration between seemingly irreconcilable enemies would have made the front pages. Today it is merely an everyday marker of the shape of things to come. I believe it indicates a new, less defensive, more open mindset that will become more and more common.

It reflects a societal shift, where power is spread and shared. And where actually the people who are the most influential are the ones who share the most, rather than the ones who try to keep control and restrict information flow.

For business, the commercial opportunities of leveraging the power of collaboration are only just starting to be explored, and those at the forefront of it will reap the benefits.

And although we no doubt won't enter a world of perfect consumption, where design meets manufacture, meets consumption, with the result being no waste, there is a massive opportunity for all businesses and leaders.

At the end of the day, we have a choice – embrace the exciting new world and be open, transparent and collaborative businesses and leaders and in doing so be more successful. Or stand by and watch people use the power of digital and social media to force us to be.

I know which option I prefer.

Summary: the power of many

▌ The social revolution will empower the consumer in the way that the Industrial Revolution empowered the corporation.

▌ Emerging mass consumption models, from Groupon to Facebook, will change the world in the same way that mass production did.

▌ Digital technology's ability to enable collaboration hasn't only changed how products are designed, produced and marketed – it's also changed how they are consumed.

▌ Think social product development, not just new product development.

▌ People today want 'more': more involvement in the design of products, more customisation and tailoring to their requirements, more responsive and connected companies.

▌ The best brains are often outside the company: collaborate with consumers, with professionals, with employees, with other companies and even with competitors.

▋ Use the power of open source, learn from the Facebooks, Groupons and Wikipedias of the world and their open, transparent and collaborative models.

▋ The same power of collaborative movements to unite behind causes will also be used against your brand or business if you don't act in the way today's prosumers and Millennials want you to.

▋ The desire to consume better has greatly driven people's focus on conscientious consumption: if 'own' was the word for the twentieth century, then 'share' will be the word for this century.

▋ The leaders and companies that understand and leverage the enormous potential of collaboration that the digital era enables will have very bright futures.

6

A new idea for a new era: the Social Business Idea™

Nothing is as powerful as an idea whose time has come.

Victor Hugo

I f you are still reading, it's most probably because you buy into the idea that consumers are driving business to be more socially responsible; that they want to know the purpose behind your business beyond just profit; that there is a major opportunity for you to out-behave your competition; and that in the world of radical transparency, where people can find out everything about your company or brand and share it with one another, the consequences of not doing could be extremely dire. And that above all, rather than just doing good because it's the right thing to do, you will actually make more money and be a more profitable business in the long run if you do.

Deciding to act is a critical step. But the key challenge, once a business has decided to act, is to identify and define what it should do, how it should act and where. In certain respects, this is much harder than taking the decision to be more socially responsible.

The answer comes from looking at the overlap between what the company is good at and what consumers or customers are looking for. At a basic level, a company should draw a

Venn diagram that in one circle says 'What is a genuine and
credible role for the brand or business?' and in the other
circle says 'What are the real issues that consumers care
about?' (Figure 6.1). The area a company should look to play
in is at the intersection of these circles.

A lot of greenwashing and nicewashing has occurred
because companies just looked at the 'what do consumers
care about?' circle and concluded 'consumers want business
to be greener or more responsible, so we'll say that we are'.
That led to an enormous amount of the activity in the Age
of Image described in Chapter 1, with BP's little flower being
among the worst offenders, and to serious damage being
done to the overall credibility of business.

Others made the mistake of focusing on something that,
although important to the company, and a genuine and
credible role for it, was of little or no interest to consumers.
Brands are the meeting point for consumer needs and wants
on the one hand and companies' sustainable profit delivery
on the other. So, if consumers want business to be more
responsible, and business wants to continue to make money,

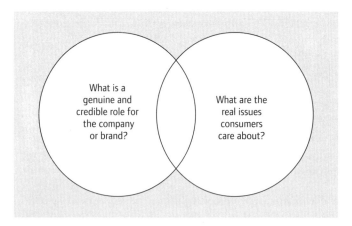

FIGURE 6.1

then it stands to reason that finding a genuine credible role for a brand that will have a positive contribution to both the world and its own profitability is the way forward.

CASE STUDY

Social Business Idea™: One Young World

One Young World is a not-for-profit global platform for the young people who will be leaders of governments and businesses tomorrow, as CNN described it, 'junior Davos'. It was created by applying the Social Business Idea process to our own business to find how we, as a company, could have a purpose beyond profit.

It is the company's tangible way of showing what can be done and comes out of the strengths and beliefs of the organisation. We specialise in creating and nurturing brands, are capable of generating high-profile media coverage and are good at organising events. We are also a leader in the digital and social media space, being one of the first in the advertising industry to comprehend open-source campaigns and recognise their incredible power.

The company vision is to be the most future-facing global ideas company and to understand more about the future of media, consumers, business and brands than anyone in our industry. Add this to my personal belief in using the power of creativity to effect positive change – the reason behind our creating and leading Kofi Annan's tck tck tck Campaign for Climate Justice or our work with UK Prime Minister David Cameron, arguably the most socially responsible leader of a major country in the world today – and One Young World is a natural conclusion.

One Young World uses elements of all those things to provide young people with a platform where they will be better placed to have an impact on the world and drive positive change. If the world's leaders can't always make the right decisions, then maybe the world's young people can help them get there. It ties in with issues people care about, it ties in with what we as a business are good at, but above all it provides an umbrella, an identity for all these inspiring young people through the open-source idea of One Young World.

At the inaugural One Young World Summit in London in 2010, we had over 800 young leaders from 114 countries, being 'counselled' by world thought leaders such as Kofi Annan, Muhammad Yunus, Desmond Tutu and Bob Geldof. One Young World 2011 in Zurich brought together more than 1,200 young people from 170 countries.

The brilliance of the delegates was humbling to all of us, and their expectation of global business was loud and unequivocal. One Young World Resolution 2010.3 reads: 'In the belief that multinational corporations have a fundamental responsibility to behave ethically, we call upon global businesses to define and act on their role in the fight against poverty and climate change.' This Resolution was passed by 81% of the delegates and supported by 98% of the thousands who were following the summit online.

These young people are the future consumers and leaders of the world. They have the means in the digital age to judge us in the business community and to make that judgement effective by giving or withholding their custom. What's reassuring is that even if the generation that is in charge now fails to capitalise on this exciting challenge, from what I saw at One Young World the next generation won't.

The two circles in Figure 6.1 on page 136 represent a good, albeit simplistic, way of defining the broad territory that a company should play in. The next step is to find the overarching idea that can be used as a strategic compass, not only to communicate this externally but also to galvanise the organisation itself.

We are living in a new world, where the rules of business and marketing have dramatically changed, where consumers and their expectations have been transformed, as has their power to act.

The social revolution has created a new era for industry. And there's a need for a new idea for this new era.

An idea that lies at the intersection of the two biggest trends impacting business today, social responsibility and social media.

An idea that allows social responsibility to sit at the heart of business strategy, not in a silo.

An idea that can be a rallying cry for the entire company.

An idea that embraces all stakeholders inside and outside the organisation.

An idea that is based on transparency and authenticity.

An idea that positions the company to deliver long-term sustainable profit growth or savings.

And above all, an idea that aligns the goals of doing well and doing good.

That idea is called the Social Business Idea™.

The Social Business Idea combines two important words that in the past century were rarely seen together but rather were viewed as coming from different worlds: 'social' and 'business'. Social Business Ideas are ideas that are inherently social, because they are good for society as a whole, not just the company. And they are business ideas because they are designed to drive profitable growth or make major savings.

We will look at some of the great examples of Social Business Ideas later in this chapter – even if they were not necessarily called that at the time they were created –

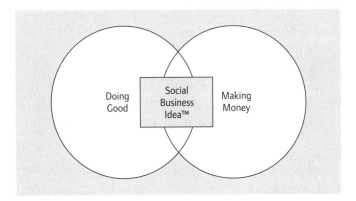

FIGURE 6.2

from Marks & Spencer's Plan A to Nike's Better World, from GE's Ecomagination to MAC's Viva Glam.

They are invariably designed to both do good and make or save money (Figure 6.2). And sometimes to do a little bit to save the planet along the way.

Defining your Social Business Idea involves a three-step analytical process, followed by a creative leap. These are the steps I go through with companies looking to put social responsibility at the heart of their businesses:

Step One

Look at all of the business stakeholders. What do they think of the company or its brands? What do they like about it and what don't they like? What is it that they are looking for from the business? What are their issues and concerns? What are the opportunities? The stakeholders are a broad group, often with quite conflicting interests. They include consumers and prosumers, both of which are ever-more influential in the digital age – especially prosumers, as they are a strong predictor of what mainstream consumers will be doing and believing in the next 6–18 months. They

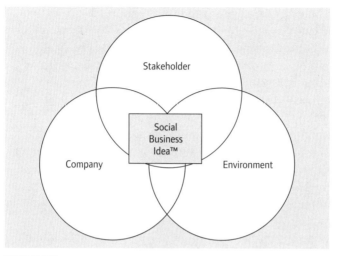

FIGURE 6.3

include employees, shareholders and the company's board of directors. At a broad and simplistic level the consumer might want more environmentally friendly and cheaper products, the shareholders may want greater profits and returns, and employees would like more money and better working conditions. The Social Business Idea resolves the conflict between these groups by finding a unifying thought that appeals to all of them. Overall, this circle helps answer the question: 'What is the issue that stakeholders care about or in essence what do people (in the broadest sense) want?'

Step Two

Do a thorough analysis of the company itself. This includes looking at the brand, or brands, and the company behind the brand. Consumers today aren't interested only in the products they buy; they are also interested in the beliefs and behaviour of the bigger entity behind those products. What is the company's history? Why was it originally founded? How has that evolved over time? What are the company and brand key awareness and image measures and relative positions versus its competitors? How does it perform on key CSR and sustainability measures? What are the core beliefs of the business or brand? And how is it delivering on them both in perceived and real terms? What is the reality of its products and services? How does it use social media? As part of this analysis we look at both the company's overall Brand Momentum and its Social Momentum. Brand Momentum asks a simple question – is the company or brand gaining or losing ground against its competitors? Brand Momentum has its origins in political polling – and our Brand Momentum studies accurately predicted the outcome of both the 2009 US election and the 2011 UK general election. They also predicted the arrival of Google as a major force. The basic premise is that momentum is more important than absolute measures. As an example, back in 2002, when we asked the question who was the leader in the internet space, AOL was by far number one. When we turned the question to momentum and asked who is gaining and who is losing ground, AOL was at number nine, with a momentum score of -30, and Google was number one, with a momentum score of $+50$. With hindsight this looks like such an obvious conclusion, but back then AOL was the dominant player and Google was on very few people's radars. Social Momentum looks at the sentiment of what is being said about the company and its brands in social media by the various stakeholders and the difference between the positive and negative sentiment and relative change over time. Interestingly, we found in the UK election that the live real-time Social Momentum data mirrored very closely the YouGov 4000 people 'real-world' polls we were doing. Overall, this circle answers the question: 'What is a genuine and credible role for the company or brand?'

Step Three

The third circle is environment. This is much broader than the 'green' side of environment, although that is an important part of it, and it is broader than just the category in which the company operates. What is the overall environment in which the business is operating, from political, to legal, to competitive, to financial? What are the constraints and opportunities provided by each of these areas? We also use semiotics, the study of visual and verbal communication and cultural codes, and specifically a tool called Decipher to look at and analyse the codes of communication in a category, to understand where and how individual brands are communicating and to help us decode category conventions to identify fresh evidence of a new way of thinking. Social Decipher replicates this but by pulling from social media and the internet rather than just from popular culture or paid-for advertising.

This circle sets out to answer the question: 'Given the overall environment in which the company operates – e.g. what the competitors are doing, what legislation exists, financial requirements – what is the tangible opportunity?

After each of these steps is carried out, we arrive at a concise summary statement for each of the three circles. Based on these clear summaries of what stakeholders want, what the business can genuinely deliver and what the tangible opportunity is, a number of potential strategic ideas are generated. These ideas are designed to play to each of the insights agreed upon for each of the overlap areas. They are then tested internally and with external audiences until the single most powerful idea is articulated and agreed: the Social Business Idea.

CASE STUDY

Social Business Idea™: Dulux Let's Colour

Working with AkzoNobel brand Dulux, Havas created a Social Business Idea, called Let's Colour. This serves many purposes for the business. The creative idea is based on the notion of regeneration through colour and was inspired by a local initiative in Brazil, where the brand, known as Coral there, had been involved in community painting projects in deprived areas. Recognising the incredible power of colour and its ability to transform, the community-based painting projects were extended globally, galvanising support through social media and commercialising the events themselves, involving retail partners and local stakeholders.

The strategy addresses multiple issues for Dulux, both internally and externally. First, it lifts the brand out of a category that is filled with paint brands executing clichéd advertising. Next, it gives the brand a global 'thought', of particular importance to the decentralised marketing structure of AkzoNobel, compounded by its 2008 £8 billion takeover of ICI, owner of Dulux.

A central idea that local stakeholders can buy into, regardless of the diverse local consumer mindsets, aligned with action they can take part in and activate locally, is clearly helping to unify Dulux and AkzoNobel, both from a market perspective and from an operational perspective.

If a Social Business Idea such as Let's Colour is going to be successful, then it is essential that the company's leader believes in it. Tex Gunning, member of AkzoNobel Executive Committee, responsible for decorative paints, has long felt strongly about the responsibility of business to play a wider, positive role in society and has been a driving force behind Let's Colour. But it is equally important that it is understood by AkzoNobel's internal audience. If employees do not grasp such initiatives to enhance the brand, differentiate it from the competition, and allow the business to do good and make money at the same time, then the initiatives will not work or be sustainable.

Social media doesn't only impact on consumer businesses and external media; it also impacts on employees and shareholders, and social responsibility drives social media from brand to employee, to prosumer, to consumer, who acts as an advocate for the brand, creating a perpetual cycle.

The Dulux Let's Colour projects, which have taken place in Rio, London, Paris and Jodhpur in India, have been a stunning success, transforming communities and generating a life of their own through social media. One project where a tenement building in Paris was painted was so well received that the local residents asked to continue with further work themselves.

The Let's Colour events are filmed and distributed, and a series of longer documentaries has been made. These are real projects, making positive things happen in communities in need, but they are also commercial events. Consumers have no problem understanding this. In some ways it can be easier for them to accept business being involved in this type of project when the commercial upside is apparent. They don't object, and Let's Colour social media activity is now inundated with requests from individuals and local groups for Let's Colour to come to their own areas – proof that social responsibility drives social media.

the best Social Business Ideas leverage the power of social media with the clarity of a socially responsible business mission

The best Social Business Ideas leverage the power of social media with the clarity of a socially responsible business mission, such as One Young World and Dulux Let's Colour. Below I describe what for me are some of the best examples of Social Business Ideas, which I didn't do but I wish I had – there are many more great examples of the concept and I'm sure you have your own views.

1. MAC: Viva Glam, featuring Lady Gaga

The Viva Glam cosmetics range was established in 1994 to support the global concern and movement for HIV/AIDS. All proceeds go to the MAC AIDS Fund, and it has so far raised $190 million, and with it MAC has created a movement. Lady Gaga has been the face of Viva Glam for two years. The 2010 campaign with Lady Gaga and Cyndi Lauper was Viva Glam's most successful ever. Lady Gaga is an inspired choice for MAC, heavily into philanthropic and charitable endeavours and by far the most connected star on social media – over 10 million Twitter followers and over 40 million Facebook fans – and with an intuitive understanding of her market. She is able to mobilise vast numbers of fans – she calls them 'Little Monsters' – and uses innovative, collaborative methods, such as asking fans to vote for which charity she should give money to. The launch day of her Viva Glam lipstick ad campaign alone generated nearly 20 million unique views in traditional media, including print and web buys, an appearance on *The Today Show* and social-media hits.

2. Levi's: Water<Less

In 2007 Levi's undertook an assessment of the real impact of its products so that it could create a meaningful sustainability programme. Water impact was clearly a major issue – a pair of Levi's 501s uses more than 3000 litres of water during its product lifecycle – this includes use during cotton growth and customer washes. The water used in the finishing process was identified as an area that Levi's controlled and could be addressed. As a result, Levi's produces jeans that it calls Water<Less, which use much less water in the finishing process. The social media aspect is very interesting, with a Levi's Water<Less Facebook page and a counter showing the total litres of water saved since the brand launched. Levi's is

donating 200 million litres of water to developing communities across the world, raised through its WaterTank competition, which encouraged users to save water for prizes or be active on social media to raise awareness of the global water shortage. The 200 million litres target was achieved.

The WaterTank app used game mechanics to educate and challenge people to make small actions to increase awareness of the global water crisis and what they can do to help. Completed challenges 'unlock' up to 200 million virtual litres of clean drinking water, representing Levi's contribution to Water.org. Users could play for fun or register with the app to play for prizes, including a trip to a community that has been helped by Water.org.

Levi's social media campaign around its new Water<Less jeans generates four times as much buzz around the brand's socially responsible image compared with normal Facebook posts.

3. Marks & Spencer: Plan A

As mentioned in Chapter 1, Marks & Spencer launched Plan A in 2007, making 100 commitments to tackle climate change, waste, raw materials, fairness throughout its supply chain and health issues over five years to 2012. The idea was that if the world didn't sort out the big issues such as climate change, then there was no Plan B. They anticipated investing £200 million over the period to achieve these targets but, according to its 2010 'How We Do Business' report, the plan had already broken even. In 2010 it added £50 million in profit and in 2011, £70 million. The M&S Plan A website informs, engages and encourages involvement, and M&S maintains a constant dialogue with consumers via Twitter about anything to do with the company, including Plan A.

4. Nike: Better World

This is a powerful initiative under the umbrella 'Our mission is to make the world better through sport'. It collates all of

Nike's social good activities, such as Considered Design, Trash Talk, the N7 Collection, and Lace Up Save Lives, and all of their broader initiatives, such as using recycled polyester, water-based cementing and environmentally preferred rubber, which is in use on the new Nike Free TR Fit.

The information is brought together on a website and communicated through a TV campaign, which, with beautiful logic, is made entirely from recycled footage from old Nike ads. In a very inclusive approach, as previously mentioned in Chapter 5, it views 'anyone with a body' as being an athlete.

5. American Express: Members Project

This major initiative solicits Amex card members to submit and vote on ideas for humanitarian projects. Launched in 2007, more than 400,000 people registered to participate and 1190 projects were submitted that year. Members vote on which charities win funding. In the past year, winning charities won funding totalling over $4,200,000 from American Express. As of 31 May 2011, the project will be moving entirely from its microsite to Facebook, where more than 800,000 people already 'like' it. It also now incorporates volunteering – give an hour – and give-a-dollar campaigns, the focus being on small steps making a difference. Members are encouraged to volunteer, earn and donate membership points and share stories.

6. Unilever: Dove Campaign for Real Beauty

This was created in 2004 and based on a global study on the perceptions and attitudes of women with regard to their personal beauty and wellbeing. The Campaign for Real Beauty was revolutionary in the category, because for the first time it showed real women rather than perfect models in its advertising. Unilever says it is much more than pure product marketing. It strove to challenge stereotypes set by the beauty industry and help women feel more positive about themselves. The Dove Evolution film, which tracks the makeup, photo retouching and technical wizardry that the beauty industry routinely employs when producing marketing materials, is one of the longest-lived viral films and a real social media success. Since its launch in 2006 it has been viewed by in excess of 23 million people, in various forms, and is still regularly viewed and shared today, five years later.

7. Pepsi: Refresh

The Pepsi Refresh project asks people to nominate and vote for community projects to effect positive change. The company expects to sponsor thousands of local initiatives, with grants ranging from $5000 to $250,000. Over 12,000 projects to date have received more than 76 million votes from the US public. These are consumer-generated ideas, but Pepsi has driven conversation by collaborating with celebrities and popular culture influencers to generate their own ideas, aimed at inspiring young people to create ideas. Nominations can be made on the dedicated Pepsi Refresh website, www. refresheverything.com, which is filled with information and film about projects that have been supported, sometimes direct from the grantees. There are also discussion spaces and a challenge section where Pepsi poses questions and asks the community to come up with solutions, such as 'How can you use art to energise a community?' A Facebook page informs, updates and calls users to action, asking them to submit ideas and vote, as does a Twitter stream, and people whose projects are up for grants use Twitter effectively to mobilise voters.

Pepsi monitors conversations, provides real-time responses and harnesses key contributors; there have been more than 2 million online comments. Interaction with refresheverything.com significantly increased brand attributes, including favourability, intent and trust, along with intent to purchase among Millennials.

8. The Body Shop

This is a company that, over the years, has been a living breathing example of a Social Business Idea. It was one of the first to prohibit the use of ingredients tested on animals and one of the first to promote fair trade with developing countries. As its website states: 'In 1985, in its first year as a public company, The Body Shop sponsors posters for Greenpeace. A year later, it creates an Environmental Projects Department of its own, while the first major window campaign for The Body Shop is "Save the Whale" with Greenpeace, in 1986. The first Community Trade product for The Body Shop, a Footsie Roller, is produced in 1986 by a supplier in southern India. This trade in Footsie Rollers has evolved into the current trade with Teddy Exports in India, a key Community Trade supplier ... In 1990 The Body Shop Foundation is established, a charity which funds human rights and environmental protection groups. The Big Issue paper for homeless people, which began as a The Body Shop Foundation project, is launched in 1991.'

By 2004, the Body Shop had 1980 stores, serving over 77 million customers throughout the world. On 17 March 2006, L'Oréal bought Body Shop for £652 million. Answering critics, founder Anita Roddick said she 'sees herself as a kind of "Trojan horse" who by selling her business to a huge firm will be able to influence the decisions it makes'. Interestingly, their refillable bottle initiative was nothing to do with recycling and more to do with the fact they couldn't afford to get loads of bottles at the start – an early example of saving money and saving the environment.

9. Groupe Danone: Grameen Danone

As mentioned in Chapter 4, this business brainchild of Muhammad Yunus, founder of the Grameen Bank, and Franck Riboud, chairman and chief executive of Groupe Danone, provides fortified yogurt to malnourished Bangladeshi children. The Grameen Danone company is integrated into the local community, rather than importing products that are mass produced elsewhere. It buys milk from local farmers, which is brought to a local factory and then mixed with other locally grown ingredients. Nutrients are added to the yogurt, some of which is sold through local shops but much of it by a network of local women.The yogurt is produced using solar and biogas energy and uses eco-friendly packaging. The 10-year plan for the business is to create more than 50 plants and several hundred jobs. The idea is to create local ecosystems. In terms of social media the project has a community of fans, investors, activists and advocates. The business informs them of what it learns in the field. The internet is the key medium for dialogue with them as it is 'interactive, transparent, and social'.

10. General Electric: Ecomagination

Giving GE a great, easily understood focus, this programme to develop clean technologies for the future has received $5 billion investment in its first five years but has generated $70 billion. It was launched in 2005. The revenue comes from products such as wind turbines and electric car charging ports, which are Ecomagination tagged products. In the next five years, GE expects Ecomagination sales to grow twice as fast as the rest of the company. It intends to open up Ecomagination to more people outside GE and outside the USA. It is now using social media to build a movement called Tag Your Green, which launched in late 2010 and aims to spread the word about living a more environmentally conscious lifestyle and make being green fun and social. It invites people to take part in challenges, some involving celebrities, to make videos, take pictures and create stories and ideas and share them with each other on YouTube, Flickr, Twitter, Howcast and Foursquare. The Foursquare element, for example, invites people to visit tagged locations to explore places that are implementing sustainable practices.

11. WWF: Earth Hour

Earth Hour began in 2007 in Sydney as a partnership with the *Sydney Morning Herald*, when 2.2 million residents of the city switched off all non-essential appliances for one hour. The following year many other cities joined in. Now it has become a worldwide event, with thousands of cities participating and major landmarks being darkened for the hour, including Big Ben, the Empire State Building, the Eiffel Tower, the Brandenburg Gate and the Forbidden City. It has become an environmental movement, uniting people around the world – the switching off, in a way, symbolises a vote by ordinary people aimed at informing world leaders of how people really feel about the issue. The movement has its own Facebook page and YouTube channel and uses other social media platforms. It generates vast amounts of earned media – before switch-off and after switch-off pictures, often striking and moving, are widely circulated, encapsulating the connected humanity across the world. It's the largest ever voluntary action movement.

12. RED

RED was founded in 2006 with a simple goal to turn the collective power of consumers into a financial force to help others in need. It works by partnering with iconic brands to create RED products – there have been many examples, from Apple's RED iPod (there have been five generations of these) to a RED American Express card, to a range of Gap products. Other partners include Dell, Motorola, Nike, Converse and Starbucks. The *Independent* newspaper even published an issue edited by Bono that was branded RED. Up to 50% of all profits go to the Global Fund for HIV/AIDS; to date $170 million has been raised and 7.5 million people impacted by the programmes. RED also leverages the power of social media: Google, Facebook and Twitter all showed their support during

World AIDS Day in 2010 by turning their home pages red and, in the case of Twitter, turning 550,000 tweets red. 'Join RED' also has a dedicated YouTube channel that has received over 5 million views.

13. Starbucks: Shared Planet

Starbucks frames this as a 'commitment' to do business in ways that are good for people and the planet. Rather than put what might be classed as CSR activity into a discrete silo, it has put it at the heart of business strategy – registering in the mind of the consumer the idea that this is a philosophy at the core of what Starbucks is about. It produces a report that defines in a transparent way exactly the progress – good or bad – that has been made in numerous areas. It focuses on three main categories: ethical sourcing, environmental stewardship and community involvement. It is also used as a platform to engage with customers on social media by posting conversation-provoking films such as a coffee buying trip that shows relationships with growers, the emphasis on buying practices and sustainability.

14. Whole Foods Market: Whole Foods – Whole People – Whole Planet

Whole Foods is now the world leader in organic and natural foods, with more than 300 stores across the USA, Canada and the UK. But its mission extends far beyond the products it sells. As well as searching for the least processed, purest food, it also operates a decentralised culture, focused on fairness, whereby staff are highly motivated.

Whole Foods' broader goal to help take care of the world while it does business means it is involved in supporting organic farming and sustainable agriculture. Its Local Producer Loan Program is an expression of this philosophy. Launched in 2007, it has funded a total of $5 million in low-interest loans to help small independent producers expand their businesses and bring more of their high-quality local products to market, which also helps create a unique experience in each store.

As proof of the importance of social media in successful socially responsible businesses, the company's main Twitter handle has more than 2 million followers.

15. Sydney Water: Tap

Sydney Water's goal is to deliver high quality water with the lowest environmental impact possible. So, in order to encourage more people to choose tap water over bottled alternatives and show tap water is kinder to the environment and a lot cheaper, it created the brand tap™, and marketed it like any other water brand. Ads ran in newspapers, magazines and on outdoor sites. The city's cafés were enlisted to support the campaign. A social media campaign built a community, and a range of clever PR and experiential initiatives ran: for example 'tap' stickers were created so people could brand their own bottles.

Whether you share my passion for Social Business Ideas or not, whether you think there are better ways of articulating the concept, what is irrefutable today is that consumers want brands and business to be more socially responsible.

We still tend to talk about social media and social responsibility as two separate and unrelated things. To reiterate my view stated in Chapter 1, I believe they are totally connected and that, far from being separate things, social responsibility actually drives social media.

The Social Business Idea is the concrete product of this belief.

Many of the most visionary business leaders – the green-blooded capitalists – are taking their companies and organisations down this path, creating their own Social Business Ideas – even if they don't know that that is what they are called – and many more will follow, sometimes despite their boards' or shareholders' views.

> **I firmly believe that not only is it possible for making money and doing good to be aligned but also that they need to be**

I'm extremely optimistic about the future of business. I firmly believe that not only is it possible for making money and doing good to be aligned but that they need to be, to ensure that social responsibility and better business become mainstream.

This is not just a great thing for business – it is a good thing for the world.

Summary: Social Business Ideas™

A Social Business Idea:

- sits at the heart of business strategy, not in a silo;
- is a rallying cry for the entire company;
- embraces all stakeholders inside and outside the organisation;
- operates at the intersection of social responsibility and social media;
- is based on transparency and authenticity;
- positions the company to deliver long-term sustainable profit growth or savings;
- aligns the goals of doing well and doing good.

The future: making a decent profit

Sometimes it falls upon a generation to be great. You can be that great generation.

Nelson Mandela

believe that we, as a generation of business leaders and practitioners, have a unique opportunity. An opportunity to demonstrate to the world that business can be a force for good. To show the potential for socially responsible businesses to bring about change – and not only because it's the right thing to do, but also because it will actually lead to better performance for our companies.

It's an incredible time for the world and it's an incredible time for business. Revolution is not a word to be used lightly. But one is taking place right now that in my view is every bit as significant as the Industrial Revolution. It's changing society. It's changing government and politics. It's challenging the legal systems around the world. It's changing how consumers think and behave. It's changing people and their understanding of their power to support the things they like and object to what they think is wrong.

At the heart of this revolution are digital technology and social media – from the Arab Spring of 2011 to Wikileaks, from the election of President Obama, to the superinjunctions in the UK, to the way the world learnt about Osama bin Laden's death – they are creating a world of radical transparency and enabling ordinary people to voice the ways in which they want the world to change.

> **in 100 years children will learn about the digital and social revolution in the same way that we learnt about the Industrial Revolution**

In 100 years – if children still go to school – they will learn about the digital and social revolution in the same way that we learnt about the Industrial Revolution.

If this revolution is changing the world, then it's also changing the world of business. Things often shift suddenly and dramatically under our noses, almost without us being aware of it, and quite quickly something becomes seen as normal that at some point wasn't. And that's exactly what's happening now.

For those people who think that business is safe and secure and doesn't need or will not be forced to change, consider this statement from W. C. Heuper at the National Cancer Institute made in 1954: 'If excessive smoking actually plays a role in the production of lung cancer, it seems to be a minor one.' It was only slightly before this that Camel had been running ads proudly proclaiming that more doctors smoked Camel than any other cigarette.

It's easy to be dismissive of the comment above as being from the last century and ridiculously out of date – but most people would not have believed a decade ago that smoking would be banned from bars and restaurants in most major cities around the world – a demonstration not only of the speed of change, but also of the power of legislation. This, incidentally, is why I personally believe legislation and not only the efforts of businesses and individuals is needed to fix the climate issue – but that is a subject for a separate debate.

Now clearly I'm not suggesting for one minute that all business is as socially irresponsible as the tobacco industry. But what I am suggesting is that accepted norms can change remarkably quickly and that following the financial and economic meltdown, in a world driven by the social consumer and some inspirational leaders, business is going to change dramatically, quickly.

The people are revolting

As we have covered in the previous chapters, the biggest driving force not only behind the majority of change we are seeing today, but also behind the change we will see in the future, is the new social consumer and its two major subsets: the prosumers – the proactive, influential consumers – and the Millennials – the young digital natives.

Prosumers have always been key in driving change, but social media has given them the power to effect change and influence many more people than in the analogue era. And today's young people, the Millennials, really are a unique generation. The digital revolution has made them completely different from any generation that has gone before. Because of technology, they are the best-informed generation of young people that the world has ever seen. And through social media they have a huge ability to influence and drive change. They are also different in that they believe that it is the duty of their generation to change the world. In the 2010 global study of Millennials mentioned in Chapter 1, a massive 84% of them believed this, and in China, arguably the most important country for the future of the world, that figure actually rises to 90%.

Following the financial and economic meltdown, we are seeing new trends. People are redefining value, looking for it more and more – they are buying cheaper products and trading down or delaying purchases. But these are, in my view, short-term trends.

The bigger-picture trends are being driven not by the recent recession, but by the needs and wants of prosumers, and especially by the new Millennial generation.

So how will the Millennial generation shape and form the future of the world?

The key thing I have seen, both from all of the global research we have done and through my work with One Young World, is how considered and mature this generation is. They are not the rebellious idealists of previous generations, they are the most socially responsible generation that has likely ever existed. It is their voice that is accelerating the global movement towards a more socially responsible future.

One of the questions is how will this generation evolve?

There are some who say their sense of responsibility is driven by the optimism of youth and that as they settle more into careers, relationships, families and 'breadwinning' they will change and become more cynical and resigned. I don't agree with this. I think the reason for their sense of social responsibility is actually that the digital revolution has given them a much greater awareness of the gravity of the issues facing the world today and the need to act. They are far more concerned than they are optimistic. They are aware of the global systemic risk – of issues such as climate change and the threat to the world's financial system. And because of how connected they are, they know their peers around the world share the same concerns and this in turn serves to exacerbate them. In the same global study carried out in

2010 in China, India, the USA, the UK and France, 74% of young people believed the world will be more dangerous and 79% believed it will be more polluted in 20 years.

We are seeing the proof of this sense of responsibility felt by the Millennials with entrepreneurs such as Adam Braun from Pencils of Promise who are putting their money where their mouths are and spurning much more financially rewarding careers for more emotionally rewarding ones. I think they will retain a shared sense of identity and purpose, being a generation with a mission to drive change in the world – like those who came of age in the 1960s or during the Second World War.

These young people are part coercing, part inspiring their seniors to act. And many are following.

As Kofi Annan said when addressing the delegates at One Young World 2010: 'From what I have seen and what I have heard in this room I know that your generation will do a much better job than mine.'

Past performance is no guarantee of future success

Yes, there are a number of questions business leaders have. Will my customers and consumers really reward me for this? Will my board? Will my shareholders?

I fundamentally believe they will. The danger of being one of the companies punished in the Age of Damage is much greater than the challenge of changing to be a better business. 'Past performance is no guarantee of future success' is the disclaimer written across every piece of communication from the financial services industry over the past decade, and nowhere is that more true than for the future of the world of business.

Already major and substantial progress is being made.

A generation of visionary leaders has understood the need and opportunity for change. People I would call the 'green-blooded capitalists' are leading this revolution.

The green-blooded capitalists

The business benefits from doing this are not soft ones about reputation or image. They are hard measures of growth and margin improvement. Wherever you look, it's a no-brainer.

Paul Polman, CEO, Unilever

You can either take the front or the back edge of this trend – of business actively engaging in these crucial issues. But I'd say that the risks are far bigger if you stay on the back edge.

John Replogle, CEO, Seventh Generation, and former CEO, Burt's Bees

Businessmen who focus on profits wind up in the hole. For me, profit is what happens when you do everything else right.

Yvon Chouinard, founder, Patagonia

The power of transformation isn't in somebody else's hands; it's in ours.

Jeffrey Swartz, CEO, Timberland

An ethical business can be profitable business and we have proved it here now quite categorically.

Sir Stuart Rose, former chairman and CEO, Marks & Spencer

I do not believe maximising profits for the investors is the only acceptable justification for all corporate actions. The investors are not the only people who matter. Corporations can exist for purposes other than simply maximising profits.

John Mackey, CEO, Whole Foods

People today want to work for a company with a purpose. And it's not just a job. It's not just a paycheque. I want to know that when I'm going to work, and I'm putting in hours, that there really is something important there ... I think we change the world by having a positive impact, community by community, city by city, product by product.

Mike Duke, CEO, Walmart

Performance with purpose doesn't mean subtracting from the bottom line. It means we bring together what is good for business with what is good for the world.

Indra Nooyi, CEO, PepsiCo

Ecomagination is not meant to revamp the brand at all; it's about good business sense. It's not an advertising ploy or marketing gimmick; GE wants to do this because it is right, but also we plan to make money while we do so.

Jeffrey Immelt, CEO, General Electric

In this ever-changing society, the most powerful and enduring brands are built from the heart. They are real and sustainable. The companies that are lasting are those that are authentic.

Howard Schultz, CEO, Starbucks

> I want to work for a company that contributes to
> and is part of the community. I want something
> not just to invest in. I want something to believe
> in.
>
> Anita Roddick, founder, The Body Shop

Yes, they want to do good, but they also want to do well.

They share a belief that being a successful business and
being a responsible business are not mutually exclusive.

One of the most exciting and encouraging things is that
the majority of these leaders are actually running large
companies. So whereas in the past good intentions were
something reserved for NGOs and small niche businesses,
today it is some of the largest corporations in the world that
are leading the way. And clearly, the bigger you are, the
bigger a positive impact you will be able to have.

As I said in Chapter 1, you can't share a loss, but the better
you do, the more good you can do. Given the sheer scale of
some global corporations and how well run they are, their
potential to have a positive impact is enormous.

As these leaders show the way and are supported by the
likes of Warren Buffett and Bill Gates with their very public
philanthropy or the new social entrepreneurs with their
business models built on openness and transparency – the
rest of the business world will follow.

> you too can seize the opportunity to out-
> behave your competition – but only if you
> beat them to it

You too can seize the opportunity to out-behave your competition – but only if you beat them to it. Find your Social Business Idea™ before they find theirs!

Not only will the most socially responsible businesses do better because consumers will reward them and become powerful advocates for their brand and businesses, but they will also do better because the best talent will want to work for them.

The concept of 'employalty' will become increasingly important in the future as a new generation of workers bring their values to the work place – loyalty to companies will be driven less and less by financial incentives and rewards and more and more by shared values and pride in the social contribution an organisation is making. I was talking with a Harvard University professor recently, who said that the majority of his smartest students no longer wanted to go into banking or business or law but wanted to join organisations such as Teach For America, because working for an organisation that is doing good has become as important to them as making money. In fact, 70% of Millennials equate a successful career with doing work that is meaningful to them. This was also the number-one ranking factor above 'higher pay' in the Future of Millennial Careers survey carried out by Harris Interactive.

The biggest barrier

A crucial factor on the road to a more socially responsible future is going to be the action and evolution of the investment and shareholder communities. The optimistic hope that the world of finance would learn from the lessons of the financial and economic meltdown is evaporating. The financial community has stalled, sticking to an old model that is focused on the latest quarter's earnings rather than sustainability and social responsibility.

Their main concerns seem to be the size of profits rather than whether those profits are sustainable – how good they feel about this year's bonus, rather than how good they feel about their contribution to a better world. As my boss, and one of France's most successful entrepreneurs, Vincent Bolloré, said about the bonuses paid to certain parts of the banking sector: 'If you drive a lorry full of gold through the middle of a city, unfortunately you are going to attract some of the wrong people.'

For now, quarterly performance is still the dominant barometer for share price movement. And sustainable or socially responsible business doesn't have the tangible positive effect in 12 weeks in the way that a merger or acquisition announcement can. But this shouldn't, and increasingly doesn't, mean that the most responsible businesses don't have better share price performance.

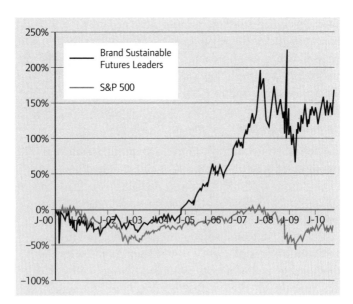

FIGURE 7.1

A study carried out as part of Havas Media's Brand Sustainable Futures demonstrated that over a 10-year period, those companies viewed as the most sustainable have actually outperformed the S&P 500 (Figure 7.1).

There is no question that a lack of social responsibility has a negative effect – just track BP's share price post-Deepwater Horizon spill for proof. I believe that business has reached a tipping point here. Consumers want it, business leaders are starting to push towards it, and governments are encouraging it.

Although being able to demonstrate immediate returns on socially responsible behaviour – such as the quantified over $200 million that Walmart has made by making its fleet more environmentally friendly – helps to build the financial case for doing the right thing, businesses will increasingly learn that if they are not genuinely being good global citizens, then people will find them out. They will be exposed and their investors will lose money.

I believe we will see major progress in ratings and metrics to measure responsible business and sustainability so that we will never have a return to the ridiculous situation where BP topped many of those rankings.

On that subject Puma recently unveiled a report that, for the first time, puts a financial value on its environmental, social and economic impact. Puma says the environmental profit and loss or EP&L report sets 'a new standard in corporate environmental reporting'. By using a system where a financial value of its impacts is calculated, Puma says the implications of its business decisions will be clearer. And, it can also be used as a way to link doing business in the right way with commercial benefits.

In the report itself, carbon dioxide (CO_2) was valued at €66 per tonne and water at €0.81 per metre cubed. In terms of the company's overall impact for 2010, this was calculated to be €94.4m with greenhouse gases contributing €47m or 49.8% and water €47.4m or 50.2%. Puma chairman and CEO Jochen Zeitz, who is also chief sustainability officer for Puma's parent company, PPR, says: 'The EP&L statement is a milestone in Puma's mission to become the most desirable and sustainable sports lifestyle company in the world. It is an essential tool and shifts how companies can and should account for and integrate the true costs of their reliance on ecosystems into business models.'

Companies such as Unilever, Motorola, Dell and GE have changed or evolved their reporting or forecasting cycles to try to wean the financial analysts off their quarterly-results addiction.

I believe we will increasingly see genuine proof emerge that doing good and doing well are intrinsically interlinked and that the best-performing stocks over time will come from the most responsible companies. We will see a modernisation of board and shareholder attitudes. And although some people believe we may even see the creation of a new financial exchange dedicated 100% to socially responsible business – 'the new NYSE' or should that be 'NICE'? – I actually believe we won't need to, as social responsibility in business will become a mainstream part of every business.

We will see a redefinition of social investment to include and embrace the notion of social businesses making profit.

And for me this is the key point: if we want the movement to socially responsible business to become mainstream and be sustainable, we need to show that doing good and making more profit are not mutually exclusive and that actually by doing good you will make more money.

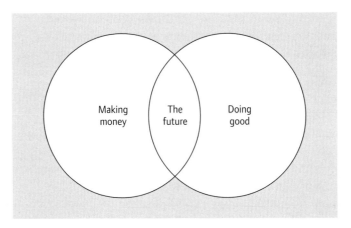

FIGURE 7.2

Doing good but not making money isn't any more sustainable a model than making money without a concern for the impact on the world around you. In my view, business must make money – or people won't do it – but it can make money in the right way (Figure 7.2).

We will increasingly see business going back to its roots, and doing good for society and the community around it.

We may even see a business leader win the Nobel Prize – in fact, Nobel should create an award to recognise those business leaders who drive major positive change in the world.

Consumers will reward those businesses and brands that stand for a purpose beyond profit; that collaborate with them rather than try to control them; that listen to them rather than talk at them; that are obsessive about having a better reality, not a better image; that put social responsibility at the core of business strategy, not in a silo. Transparency, authenticity and speed will be the rules of the game, not only for the social media world but also for the modern business. Business will be open. Business will be 'good'.

And there will be three types of business leader: those who make it happen, those who watch it happen, and those who wake up too late and wonder what happened.

Two of the biggest issues and opportunities facing all businesses today are how to cope with the dramatic rise of social media and how to be more socially responsible. As I hope I have made clear, in my view they are not separate subjects but are in fact interlinked. In the next decade, those leaders and companies that are the most socially responsible will reap huge benefits from the power of social media, as employees and consumers become powerful advocates for their brands and businesses.

I appreciate that there will be those who are cynical about the need to change, who prefer the old model of capitalism. To them I have a simple message: your model nearly caused the meltdown of the entire global economic and financial system. It is not sustainable. The train has already left the station and the world is moving on fast. Now is the time to get on board, to re-evaluate by embracing the change and embarking on an exciting new journey. There is one thing of which I am sure – you will have a better business as a result.

I believe the future of business is much more positive than cynics would like us to believe.

That we have a golden opportunity not only to make more money but also to become a force for good in the world.

To transform our companies into ones that are at the same time socially responsible and commercially successful.

To show that doing the right thing does not mean sacrificing profits and in fact is the only realistic way to ensure a sustainable return on investment.

> the most profitable and successful
> businesses will increasingly be those that
> demonstrate the ability to add value in a
> socially responsible way

In the social media age, the most profitable and successful businesses will increasingly be those that demonstrate the ability to add value in a socially responsible way. The leading businesses of the future will be powered by authenticity, transparency and speed. Any company that can't engage deftly and creatively with these drivers will be left behind.

Imagine a world where the most successful and richest people in the world got there because they had helped the most people or done the most good. Where the most profitable companies in the world were the ones that had had the most positive impact on the planet. Where the more you gave back, the more you made.

Not only would it be a great place to live, it's actually the world I believe we can create.

Index